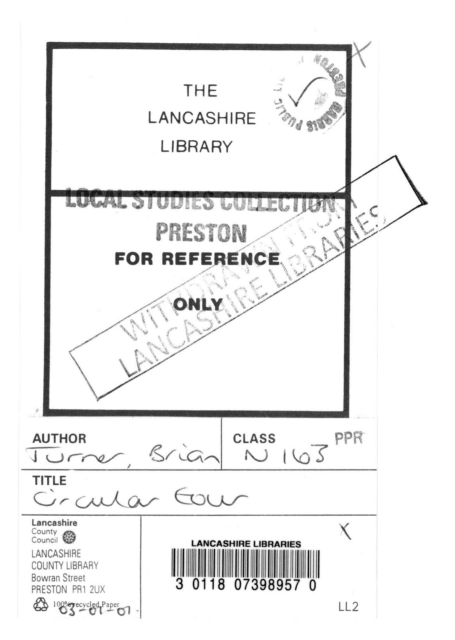

CIRCULAR TOUR

Seaside Pleasure Riding by Tram

Above: *All the fun of the toastrack - a picture that seems to capture the very essence of seaside pleasure riding by tram. Car 20, one of Llandudno's four toastracks, starts the descent of the Little Orme on 2 July 1950, heading for Colwyn Bay - despite the destination plate. (John H. Meredith)*

Front Cover: *Blackpool's first toastrack tram, No. 69, loads for the Circular Tour in Talbot Square during August 1911. (Water colour by Wayne Chapman, Mind's Eye, St. Annes)*

CIRCULAR TOUR

Seaside Pleasure Riding by Tram   BRIAN TURNER

Printed by Amadeus Press, 517 Leeds Road, Huddersfield, West Yorkshire HD2 1YJ

© Brian Turner, 1999

ISBN 0 9535763 0 2

Rio Vista

19 Norfolk Road, Lytham, Lancashire FY8 4JG

One location above all others is indelibly associated with seaside pleasure riding – Blackpool's Golden Mile. In this evocative 1935 scene, toastrack tram No. 78 is flanked by two of Blackpool's new streamlined Boat cars, with an ancient Lytham St. Annes open-topper and a new railcoach in the distance. On the carriageway, brand-new Gondola bus No. 114 is returning to Rigby Road garage, presumably for the lunch break, followed by 1928 Leyland Lion No. 61, which two years later was itself rebuilt into an open "runabout". (SD)

TOUR ITINERARY

Acknowledgements

I have relied, throughout this book, on information and illustrations from a wide range of sources, in particular:

Roy Brook, Huddersfield
Paul Class, Gales Creek, Oregon
Albert Clayton, St. Michaels
Terry Daniel, Blackpool
Jim Dean, Southport
Richard Delahoy, Southend
David Dewhurst, Blackpool
Bob Dobson, Blackpool
Eric Fielding, St. Annes
Peter Fitton, Lytham
Les Folkard, Torquay
John Fozard, Keighley
Dennis Gill, Cheadle
Karlyn Goulborn, Rhyl
Robert Haley, St. Annes

Stephen Holt, Ansdell
Fred Ivey, London
Peter Jackson, Blackpool
Stanley King, Bradford
Arthur Kirby, Bramhall
Bill Latham, Inskip
Vernon Linden, Blackpool
Ian McLoughlin, Blackpool
John Meredith, York
Michael Morton, Blackpool
Alan and Mary Murray, Carleton
Eric Old, Bangor
David Padgham, St. Leonards
David Packer, Bromley
Martin Petch, Southampton

Geoff Price, Halton-on-Lune
John and Doreen Read, Heysham
Barry Rollinson, Bridgwater
Tony Sharkey, Blackpool
Ralph Smedley, Cleveleys
Simon Smith, Scarborough
Tony Stevenson, St. Annes
Tom Stringer, Lytham
Keith Terry, Leeds
Rosemary Thacker, Crich
Glynn Wilton, Crich
Richard Wiseman, Richmond
Peter Worden, Blackburn
Jack Wyse, London

Blackpool Art Gallery
Blackpool Library
Blackpool Tourism Department
Blackpool Transport Services
Bournemouth Library
Brighton Library
British Commercial Vehicle Museum
The Gazette, Blackpool
Great Yarmouth Library

Harris Museum & Art Gallery, Preston
Hastings Library
Hulton Getty Collection
Portsmouth Library
Lancashire Record Office
Lancaster City Museum
Margate Library
Merseyside Maritime Museum
Merseyside Record Office

Morecambe Library
National Tramway Museum
St. Annes Library
San Francisco Public Utilities Division
Sankey Collection
Southport Library
Studio D
Tram 57 Project, Southampton

I am very grateful to all of them, and particularly to Ted Lightbown of the Blackpool & Fylde Historical Society. I have credited pictures to the photographer where possible, and to the source (by initials) where relevant: other items are from my own collection.

Brian Turner

Lytham, June 1999

An American tram at the English seaside. Parasols were still in vogue when this picture of Isle of Thanet car 38 was taken at Ramsgate harbour. It was one of twenty cars built by the St. Louis Car Company for the opening of the line to Margate in 1901 - the first bogie cars in the South of England. Eight-wheelers were extremely rare in the South (outside London) and these examples only lasted until 1904, being rebuilt as four-wheelers after several accidents on Ramsgate's hills. Although the Thanet line was very scenic and served two major resorts, it was one of the few South Coast tramways which never ran any sort of tourist service.

PART 1. ROUND BLACKPOOL

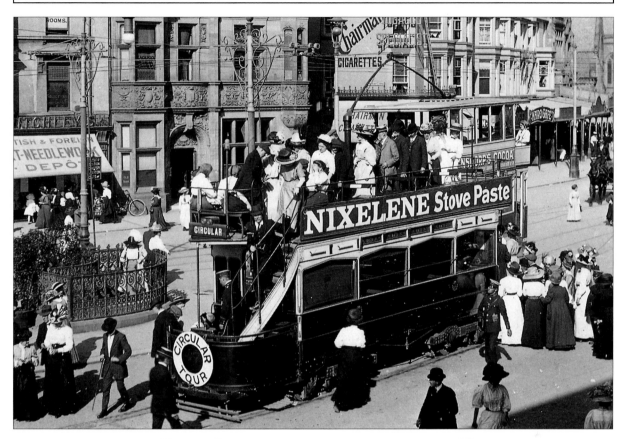

1. The Circular Tour : Rags to Riches

During the past twenty-five years or so, the notion of riding on trams purely for pleasure has become firmly established around the world. Tramways all over Europe have introduced special tourist services with preserved vehicles, whilst cities in the USA and New Zealand have built complete new tramways, operated by restored or replica trams, purely as tourist attractions.

Perhaps "re-established" would be a better word, because in the days before the motor car, tram-riding for fun was quite a common pastime. Many American tramways ran excursions with special tourist cars, and most of Britain's seaside tramways depended heavily on visitors riding just for the sake of it. But it's doubtful whether any tramway in the world developed pleasure riding into a more intense and commercially successful activity than Blackpool with its Circular Tour.

Blackpool had pioneered electric street tramways in 1885 and led the

Above: **As fast as one set of passengers disembarked from the Circular Tour, another car-load took their place – or rather half a car-load, as nobody wanted to travel inside when the sun was shining. (AMM)**

Below: **The circular route round Marton started with horse-buses in 1892. The service was run by a variety of local livery stables; this is John Smith's bus *The Countess* waiting by the drinking fountain at Talbot Square in 1899. (Arthur Dearden/PJ)**

field in providing holiday attractions for the working classes, so it was hardly surprising that these two strands came together and that tram-riding became a holiday feature in its own right. The surprise was that it took so long. It was 1905 before the Circular Tour first ran, but 1911 before it established itself as a major attraction, and a ride round the town on an open "toastrack" tram became a regular feature of a trip to Blackpool.

In fact the Circular Tour in its early days showed scant promise, and bore little resemblance to the operation that was from 1911 the most profitable tram route in Britain. Although the journey was much the same, everything else

Above: **When the Corporation converted the seafront line from conduit track to overhead wires in June 1899, they removed the competing Promenade horse-buses by withdrawing their licences. Only the Marton Circular buses were then allowed on the Promenade. One of them is standing just north of Church Street later that summer, with tramcar No. 5 passing on its way to Victoria Pier via Lytham Road. The left-hand track in the foreground was laid as soon as the last conduit car had run; it stretched as far as the Tower, where it joined the existing double line along the Golden Mile. The seafront route south of Central Pier remained single-track until the Promenade was widened between 1902 and 1904.** *(BL)*

Below: **A typical scene on the Marton route around 1905, with houses straggling along the east side of a tree-lined Whitegate Drive, and open fields to the west. Trees rarely grew of their own accord in Blackpool, and these originated as part of an improvement scheme during the 1890s. Although many of them succumbed to the Blackpool climate, they lasted better than in Lytham Road, where 1¼ miles of trees were planted but only three specimens survived by 1897. Motherwell car 52 is showing "Depot Only" but since the driver is not in uniform and the car is heading away from Marton Depot towards Palatine Road and the town centre, No. 52 is probably on its way to the main depot in Blundell Street.** *(R.W. Lord)*

about the 1905 Circular was different – it ran all year; it ran both ways round the route; it used ordinary trams; and it lost money.

The Circular Tour was Blackpool Corporation's response to three problems which confronted them in the early years of the century. Some of these problems arose from the uncomfortable mix of municipal and company tramways which had developed since the Corporation took over the original Promenade line from the Blackpool Electric Tramway Company in 1892.

The Marton Problem

The Corporation's worst headache in 1905 was the Marton route, which had opened between Talbot Square and Central Station – almost a full circle – in May 1901. The line ran for much of its length through open fields or thinly populated areas. The Corporation realised that there wouldn't be much residential traffic at first, but hoped that the semi-rural nature of the route would attract pleasure riders in summer. They estimated that the receipts would be £15,000 a year.

At first the plan seemed to be working. In its opening year 113,000 passengers – one in ten – rode all the way round the route. But the novelty soon wore off. "That awful Marton route loses more money than we make out of the Promenade and Lytham Road," bemoaned the *Blackpool Times* after tramway profits had fallen from £8,837 in 1900 to £1,032 in 1903. By 1905 the Marton receipts still hadn't reached

£10,000 a year – despite the route being extended in summer to Victoria Pier and Manchester Square – and pleasure riding had dropped by half.

The Charabanc Problem

Losing the tourist business was partly a result of the Corporation's cavalier attitude to the horse-bus operators who had built up the Marton route in the first place. The service had been started in 1892 by James Lucas, landlord of the Oxford Hotel, with two buses running on a circular route from Talbot Square via the Promenade, Lytham Road, Cow Gap Lane (Waterloo Road) and Whitegate Drive. By 1898 Lucas had three vehicles on the route, plus one to the Oxford Hotel only, and seven other livery stables were each running a single bus.

When the Corporation opened the Marton tramway, they eliminated the horse-bus competition by the simple expedient of withdrawing their licences; they had done the same on the Promenade in 1899. The operators kept their horses but swapped the buses for charabancs and wagonettes and started running Circular Tours into the countryside round Blackpool – charabanc rides were always "Circular" whatever the route. It's worth saying here that since the name of the vehicle itself defies any satisfactory adaptation from the original "chars-à-banc", particularly in the plural, the anglicised "charabanc" is used for simplicity.

The Lytham Problem

The Marton route wasn't the only problem facing the Corporation in the south-eastern part of the town. The Blackpool St. Annes & Lytham Tramway Company had long been a thorn in the Corporation's side, even before they opened for business in 1896. The Corporation, under duress, had agreed to lease the tramway in Lytham Road South to the Company, but refused to let them run any further north than South Shore Station.

This sort of conflict between company and municipality was becoming increasingly common, and in a similar situation in April 1904, the House of Lords ruled that the Tyneside Tramways & Tramroads Company were entitled to run over the Newcastle Corporation tramway system.

This judgment completely undermined Blackpool's position, and when the Lytham Company re-opened the offensive in September 1904, the Corporation offered them running rights to Central Station, Victoria Pier or Manchester Square, but not along the Promenade itself.

St. Michael's was a popular destination for charabancs – just far enough for a half-day trip. *(AC)*

The Company settled for Central Station all year, and the other two in summer only. From Whitsuntide 1905 the Lytham Company effectively took over the southern part of the Marton route, though the Corporation cars continued to run to Central Station.

The Circular Solution

Amongst all these problems facing the Corporation's long-serving Tramways Manager John Lancaster in 1905 there was one piece of good news. Whitsuntide would see the completion of the momentous scheme to widen the Promenade to 100 feet *(pages 8/9)*.

The project had started at Victoria (now South) Pier in 1902 and progressed in three stages towards North Pier, gradually transforming the Promenade route from a cramped and congested line – much of it single-track – into a segregated tramway as modern as any in the world.

The extra capacity of the new Promenade line allowed John Lancaster to devise a neat solution to restore the fortunes of the Marton route. Basically he took the summer service which had run from Talbot Square via Marton to Manchester Square, and extended it back up the Promenade to form a circle 4½ miles long, in effect restoring the original horsebus route. Hopefully this would appeal more to tourists than the existing Marton service, returning them safely to Talbot Square instead of dropping them 500 yards away at Central Station.

The new route ran for the first time on 10 June 1905, the start of the Whitsuntide weekend. It operated in both directions, which required a few yards of awkward wrong-line running for clockwise cars to cross into Talbot Square. Although no detailed timetable has survived, the Circular cars apparently alternated with those on the normal Marton service to Central Station and charged the same fares, with a 4d. round-trip ticket. Passengers could board at any stop.

Slow Start

This early Circular Tour made very little impact. After its first weekend, the *Blackpool Gazette* noted that "the only cars which were not filled to overflowing were those going on the circular tour round Marton, and it is evident that Mr. Lancaster will have his work cut out to make this trip a popular success."

By the July of 1905, the Circular was taking £70 a week, which rose to £160 in August but fell back to only £9 a week before the season ended in October. The disappointing receipts were partly due to confusion over the fares. Even some members of the Tramways Committee thought that the round-trip fare only applied from Talbot Square, so it was not surprising that out of almost 600,000 passengers that year, only one in twenty rode all the way.

The end of the 1905 season didn't mean the end of the Circular service –

*T*he Circular Tour could never have started in 1905 without Blackpool Corporation's far-sighted decision to spend more than £300,000 on widening the Promenade and replacing the congested street tramway with a segregated track which was years ahead of its time. The new Promenade was 1¾ miles long and eighty feet wide plus another twenty feet for the tramway.

This view along Central Beach shows the final stage of the project, which had started at Victoria Pier in May 1902 and opened to Alexandra Road in 1903, Central Pier in 1904 and eventually to North Pier in 1905. At its peak, 700 men were employed, most of them loading and carting 450,000 cubic yards of sand from the beach to fill the reclaimed land behind the new sea-wall. A constant stream of horse-drawn carts can be seen winding their way slowly off the beach, across the new tram tracks and up the Promenade carriageway towards North Pier - and back.

To augment this laborious operation at North Pier, where the Promenade reached its highest point, the Corporation built the 300-foot jetty which can be seen on the shore. An electric pump – powered from the tram supply – sucked sand and water from the beach and delivered it at the rate of 700 tons per hour through a pipe directly into the space behind the sea-wall.

The new tram tracks came into use on 20 April 1905 in time for Easter, but it was Whitsuntide before the old tracks were lifted, the temporary wooden poles removed and the junction at Talbot Square completed, ready for the start of the Circular Tour on 10 June. (Blackpool Times/VL)

Above: **The widened Promenade looks spick and span in this rare 1905 view of Motherwell car 45 on the new Circular route - with a typically meagre load. The Motherwells, named after the town where they were built in 1902, operated the route in its early years. Not having "Circular" on their destination blinds, they showed "Oxford Hotel" and the driver changed it to "North Pier" halfway round. The board on the dash reads "Marton & North Pier". The row of seats along the tram track was a short-lived feature of the new Promenade. The elegant lamp standards lasted much longer; introduced in 1893, and based on a design used in Paris, some survived until the early 1960s. On the right the Golden Mile was steadily taking over the gardens along Central Beach. The French Exhibition was a pretty mild affair - a waxworks of scenes in the streets of Paris and "a vivid reproduction of mixed bathing at Trouville", eked out by "remarkably good models of the Russo-Japanese War". It only lasted for one season.**

Below: **These two Lancaster bogie cars – again named after their birthplace – had been the largest electric trams in the world when the Corporation bought them in 1894, shortly after taking over the Blackpool Electric Tramway Company. They were frequent performers on the Circular Tour before the toastracks came. When this photograph was taken in August 1911, No. 11 had just been heavily rebuilt by the Corporation; No. 12 was still largely original.** *(AMM)*

The first two toastracks, Nos. 69 and 70, load for the Circular Tour on the new siding outside North Pier in 1911. For many years Circular cars loaded here when they switched from Promenade duties. As road traffic increased, the siding became less practical, and in 1942 it was replaced by a similar track on the west side of the line. *(AMM)*

just the opposite, in fact. The normal Marton service from Talbot Square to Central Station was replaced completely by the Circular. Central Drive was served by Lytham St. Annes cars and by a new Corporation service between Central Station and Victoria Pier.

This winter arrangement was no more successful than the summer one, and in its first twelve months the Circular earned a miserable 5.91d. per car-mile, even less than the Layton route which was usually the worst performer. The Circular was losing over £1,000 a year, which wasn't much help to the struggling Marton route. Nevertheless John Lancaster persevered with the Circular through the summer of 1906, though he closed it the following winter and restored the Marton route to Central Station.

From 1907 the Circular operated only at Easter, Whit and from July to October, and no longer ran to a timetable. It averaged about thirty trips a day according to demand, and began to make a modest contribution to the Marton route, carrying around 150,000 passengers a year, though only about 20,000 made the round trip.

Furness Takes Over

John Lancaster died in March 1910 and it looked as if the Circular would disappear with him. That year it didn't run at Easter and it didn't run at Whit. Lancaster's successor, Charles Furness, clearly saw better uses for his ageing and inadequate rolling stock.

Yet somehow the Circular managed to survive. It reappeared for a handful of trips that July, taking just £41, and a

few more in August, but stopped again at the end of the month. Then it restarted and ran fitfully until ending as usual in the first week of October. During the whole of 1910 the route earned only £263. Prospects for 1911 looked grim.

The "New Circular Tour"

But Furness had plans for the Circular. They centred on relaying the old conduit track in Station Road at South Shore and restoring its connection with the Promenade, which for some reason had been severed when the reservation was built in 1903.

A new junction outside Victoria Pier was completed during the second week of April 1911, just in time for Easter. Straight away Furness extended the Circular down the Promenade to Station Road, making the journey five miles long. This not only raised the Tour's profile with visitors on the Promenade; it also by-passed the most tedious part of the route along Lytham Road. Furness still had to use ordinary trams, but he livened them up by placing large life-belt devices on the dash panels.

Immediately after Whitsuntide 1911 the track gang started work on a new layout to reduce congestion outside North Pier. They lifted the short siding which had been laid near the Metropole Hotel in January 1903 as a terminus for the Lytham Road cars, and replaced it by a much longer double-ended siding in the carriageway alongside Talbot Square. The new layout, which would serve as the loading point for cars changing from the Promenade onto the

Circular route, was completed just in time for the Coronation celebrations on 22 June.

During the summer of 1911, helped by the best weather in living memory, the extended Circular grew more and more popular. Receipts in July were nearly £300 – more than for the whole of 1910 – and the season had only just begun. There was a lull at the start of August when every available car was diverted onto Race Specials for the opening of the racecourse at Squires Gate, but this turned out to be just a theatrical pause before Furness's big moment - the launch of the toastracks.

The Toastracks

On 7 August 1911, four new trams entered service - three De Luxe double-deckers on the Promenade and

In February 1912 the Corporation ordered 30,000 sets of picture postcards of the Circular Tour from Raphael Tuck. There were two sets, each of four cards, which the conductors on the Tour sold at 2d a set. Unfortunately this broke the town's unwritten rules on municipal trading, and following pressure from shopkeepers, the Corporation were forced to sell them off later in 1912 to a local wholesaler.

a toastrack, No. 69, on the Circular Tour. The toastrack was a sensation. During its first week the Tour took £296, and the next week - with sister car No. 70 in service - £464. Over the following month the Circular ran nearly 2,000 trips and took more money than the old route normally earned in an entire year.

The new toastracks were just the catalyst. Altogether 25 trams were operating the Tour on 2 September, only two of them toastracks. Furness was understandably jubilant: "The new Circular Tour … will turn the Marton route from a non-paying line into a very remunerative line."

So remunerative, in fact, that by autumn 1911 the Circular Tour was earning 2s. 7¾d. per car-mile, nearly double the rest of the Blackpool system, and three times the national average. The Corporation already had the second highest revenue per mile of any tramway in Britain, exceeded only by the Fleetwood Tramroad.

Even so the only routes to make a profit in 1911 were the Promenade and the Circular Tour. Marton lost £3,709. As Furness put it: "If it were not for the Promenade section, it would be impossible to keep the whole concern out of the bankruptcy court." Marton, he said, had lost £50,000 since 1901.

Since toastracks were clearly money-spinners, the Corporation ordered six more in November 1911. The Blackpool, St. Annes & Lytham Tramway Company were equally impressed, and drew up plans to buy toastracks and run a joint tour with Blackpool, but nothing came of it. The Lytham Company needed the money - their trams only earned 10d. a mile and never managed to pay a dividend.

The six new toastracks arrived in time for the re-opening of the Circular on Good Friday, 5 April 1912. An interesting episode took place the day before, when two of the new cars, 74 and 76, were used to test the realigned junction from Talbot Road into Abingdon Street, which had been too tight for the toastracks. This suggests that there were plans to run some of the Circulars via Talbot Road instead of Clifton Street, but there is no record of it ever happening.

At this time the Circular was still operating on the original basis of boarding at any stop. Residents treated the toastracks just like other trams and if there was room, they got on. Now they began to complain that the Circulars were full of visitors. To alleviate the problem, some of the journeys at Easter 1912 started from what was curiously described as "the Promenade South", which may have been the Pleasure Beach or Victoria Pier.

Wherever it was, the experiment was not thought to have been a success, and doesn't seem to have been repeated. Instead in 1913 the Corporation banned season-ticket holders from using the Circular cars at busy times, though it's doubtful how effectively the ban could have been applied, and it was relaxed in July 1916. A more successful experiment was the extension of the running season. From 1912 to 1914, the Circular started at Easter and ran right through to the end of October.

The Jackpot

The Circular had carried 248,000 passengers in 1911. In 1912 it carried 572,000, despite the wettest summer for thirty years (it rained on 24 days in June, 17 in July and 28 in August). As many as 36 cars were running at a time, including four more toastracks delivered in July that year.

Another six toastracks arrived in June 1913, not a day too soon, as the Circular Tour had been almost overwhelmed at Whit; on the Sunday thirty cars were running a 1½-minute service. With a fleet of eighteen toastracks and another fine summer, the 1913 Circular Tour soared to a level that was never to be equalled - over 700,000 passengers, with receipts of more than £10,000.

Not bad for a route that had been on its last legs just three years earlier.

Soon after the first toastracks arrived at the beginning of August 1911, Charles Furness organised a photo-session along the most scenic part of the route in Whitegate Drive. It was a painstaking affair, involving turning the trolley, seats and passengers at each location to face the light. For all their efforts, the most interesting part of this scene near Beechfield Avenue is the Motherwell car in the background, which appears to be on a clockwise Circular journey - the only known photograph of one. *(R.W. Lord/BL)*

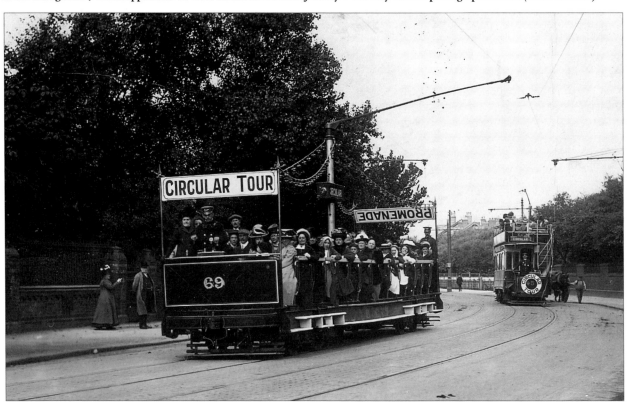

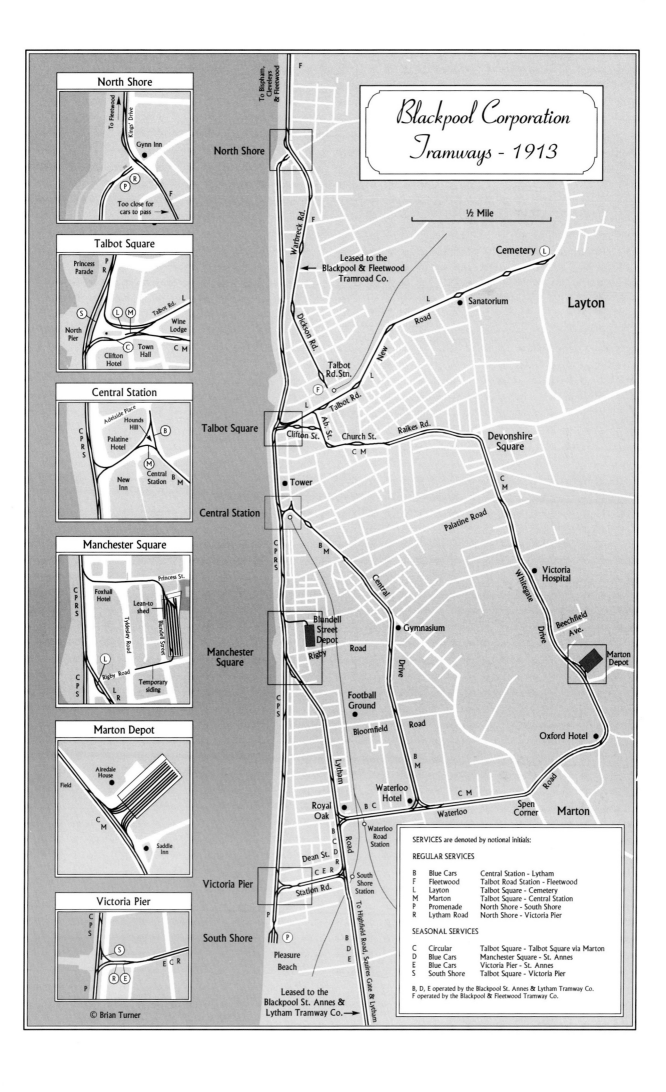

Edwardian Comings and Goings

Above: Day trippers used to carry "excursion bottles" – cheap glass hip-flasks designed to fit into the pockets of a suit or dress – which fortified them on the train and would be refilled in Blackpool for the journey home. This could explain the cheerful demeanour of this party from Manchester, newly delivered to the excursion platforms at Talbot Road Station by one of the Lancashire & Yorkshire Railway's 1500-class engines. The lady marked with the cross is Beatrice: she sent the postcard to Nellie in Scotland, saying that it wasn't a very good photograph of Harry – presumably the other cross.

Below: On Thursday 17 August 1911 – two weeks after the first toastracks appeared – the railwaymen called a national strike, stranding thousands of holidaymakers in Blackpool on the Saturday. Wagonettes and charabancs quickly capitalised on the situation, offering transport to Preston for 3s. 6d. and Blackburn for 4s. 6d. Most visitors had spent up by then, and had to find other ways of getting home. Some went by tram to Lytham and walked from there; the Lytham tramway company allowed those who had no money to travel free. The strain is showing on the weary faces of these women and children from Blackburn, who eventually found a place on one of Daniel Thwaites' steam wagons, returning from a delivery of beer to the Duke of York on Dickson Road. The men – and many women and children – had to walk with their luggage, some as far as Manchester and Halifax; there were dreadful scenes on the road to Preston, as exhausted walkers collapsed by the roadside.

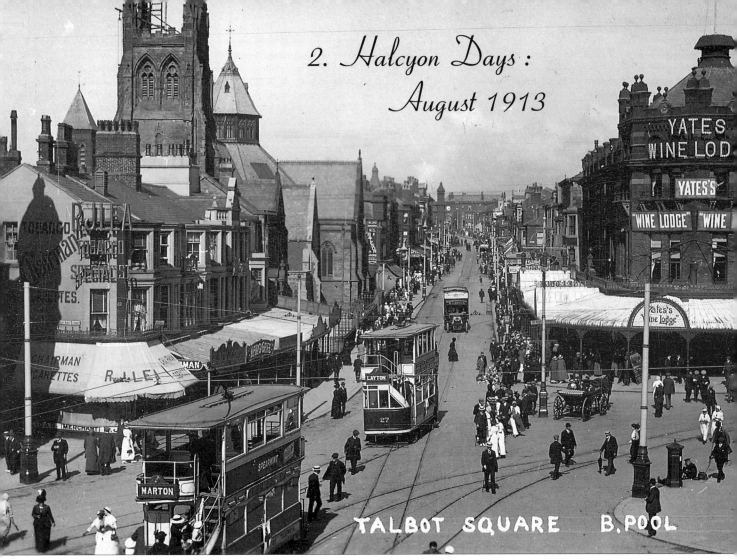

TALBOT SQUARE   B.POOL

Perhaps the best way to convey the appeal of the Circular Tour in its golden age, just before the First World War, would be to take a ride round the town on a toastrack during the busiest weekend the Tour ever had – August Bank Holiday, 1913.

1913 was a wonderful year for Blackpool in general and the Circular Tour in particular. The sun shone all through July: by August there was a hosepipe ban, and every night the Lancashire & Yorkshire Railway had to bring in a train of tank cars with water from East Lancashire to keep its local engines running.

All over Blackpool's main catchment areas in Lancashire, Yorkshire and the Midlands the textile and engineering trades were booming and the workers had money to spend. That weekend it seemed as though every one of them had set off for Blackpool. Altogether the railway companies organised 250 special excursions, on top of 300 scheduled trains already running to Blackpool during the weekend.

The first excursion arrived from Birmingham at 3.30 on Saturday morning. The staff at the Blackpool stations were struck by how many passengers were carrying wicker "dress baskets", which meant that they had

Half past three on Saturday 3 August 1913, and visitors are walking down Talbot Road from the railway station at the start of the busiest weekend the Circular Tour ever had. Marton Box car 27 is arriving from Layton, with Motherwell car 48 standing at the terminus of the Marton route, ready to set off up Clifton Street. *(RS)*

come for the weekend - if they could find somewhere to stay.

Blackpool had never been so crowded. At one three-bedroomed terraced house off Central Drive the family of four slept in the wash-house, whilst thirty visitors occupied the rest of the building. They were the lucky ones: many others had to sleep on the cliffs, amongst the sandhills or in the Promenade shelters.

Wherever they slept, they awoke on Sunday to a perfect summer's day. The sun was beating down and soon Talbot Square was thronged with perspiring holiday-makers, all dressed in their Sunday best. The men wore the regulation collar, tie and waistcoat, with the straw hats that were all the rage that summer. The ladies at least could wear something more appropriate for a hot August day. But they were all more than happy to spend 4d. for a sit down and a cooling ride on a toastrack.

Point-Boys and Step-Lifters

Not everybody was in holiday mood. Bank Holiday week was the most difficult time of the year for the

Corporation Tramways Department, who always turned out every tram they had – 78 altogether in 1913.

To operate these 78 cars for up to eighteen hours a day, the Corporation had only 85 regular drivers and 113 conductors (the Dreadnoughts and Lancasters needed two conductors). That week they had to be augmented by as many of the maintenance staff as could be spared. Since there were no cars in the workshops, the painters spent most of the week driving trams. They perhaps enjoyed the change, but wouldn't be too pleased to receive the drivers' pay of 6½d. an hour, instead of their usual 8d. Even Ted Hall, the foreman painter, had a day as an inspector, whilst the depot tailor spent half his week cleaning trams.

Most tramwaymen – there were no women - worked at least eighty hours that week. Albert Bate, for instance, did 35 hours as a bodymaker and 55 hours driving trams. John Williamson, the electrical fitter, put in 102 hours to keep the trams on the road.

Keeping trams on the road was one thing; keeping them moving was a different matter, particularly at places like

Bank Holiday visitors waiting in Talbot Square for a ride on the Circular Tour would scan the far end of Clifton Street by the Post Office for the next toastrack to appear round the corner from Abingdon Street - in this case No. 72 following Motherwell car 42 on the Marton service. Clifton Street was changing from a select residential thoroughfare into a busy commercial and shopping area, with the western end leading the process. The shop on the right was one of many in the town selling fents - remnants of cloth. *(R.W. Lord/BL)*

Talbot Square and the Pleasure Beach. Tasks which in quieter times fell to the crews became specialist functions. There were nine point-boys on duty that Bank Holiday, earning between 10s. 0d. and 15s. 0d. a week, changing the points at busy junctions and termini.

Perhaps the most specialised of these jobs - only employed during the peak season - was the "step-lifter" who raised and lowered the steps at each end as trams arrived at the Pleasure Beach terminus - no light task with the massive steps on the Dreadnoughts. Step-lifters were paid 5d an hour, the same as trainee conductors. There were two of them on duty that week – the only time this happened in 1913.

Talbot Square

Talbot Square was the official centre of the town and the place where all the Corporation tram routes met. Because Blackpool didn't go in for through-

The driver of toastrack No. 70 watches his last passengers clamber aboard in Talbot Square for another Circular Tour one sunny afternoon in August 1911. On the right, top-covered Marton Box car 27 is leaving for Marton, whilst on the north of the Square another of these ungainly vehicles – this time open-topped - has just arrived from Layton. *(AMM)*

running between routes, the layout wasn't over-complicated, but the Square was usually a hive of activity, with trams coming and going on all sides.

On the west of the Square was the paved reservation carrying the Promenade and Lytham Road routes up to North Shore and the Gynn, where passengers could change onto a Tramroad car for Bispham, Cleveleys or Fleetwood. Leading off this reservation was the siding laid in 1911 for Circular Tour cars to load when they changed from Promenade duties. The siding was also used by trams on a summer shuttle service along the Promenade to a similar siding at Victoria Pier.

On the north side of the Square was the terminus of the short route to Layton, which was Blackpool's poorest area and always got the worst cars. At least the Layton trams had been setting off from Talbot Square in style for a few weeks, passing through a large triumphal arch which had been erected at the bottom of Talbot Road for King George V's visit on 8 July. On the east of the Square a slightly better class of tramcar left from another siding for the more salubrious district of Marton.

Boarding the Tour

The only trams to cross from Talbot Square onto the Promenade were the Circular Tour cars, which loaded on the single line along the south side of the Square by the drinking fountain.

Loading a toastrack was never an exact science, and usually involved an element of "every man for himself". Passengers waited in a rudimentary sort of queue - more of a line, really. The habit of queueing wasn't acquired until the First World War, but there was a modest degree of organisation, in that passengers alighted on the off-side of the toastrack at the same time as new passengers were getting on at the near-side. In theory a toastrack could seat 69 passengers - five on each row minus one for the trolley mast - but nobody would be counting.

Central Station

As soon as a full complement of passengers had climbed, crawled or otherwise scrambled aboard, the driver would edge the toastrack carefully across the Promenade carriageway and join the main line down the paved reservation.

At quieter times the conductor would collect the fares at Talbot Square, but this August weekend he had to swing along the footboard, hanging on with one hand, taking money with the other, and somehow punching tickets. Surprisingly there's no record of a conductor falling

off, though it must have happened.

The first stretch of the Tour was downhill, past the magnificent Palace and Tower buildings to what the Tramways Department perversely referred to as "Central Station". Since the station itself was almost invisible from the Promenade, this was a curious way to identify such a prominent landmark as the Tower, but it reflected the Corporation's determination to avoid advertising places of entertainment. The Promenade route abounded with Tramways Department euphemisms - "North Shore" instead of Gynn, "Talbot Square" for North Pier, and "South Shore" for Pleasure Beach. For some reason the rule didn't seem to apply to Victoria Pier.

Whatever the name, there was a single-track junction just south of the Tower, leading across the road into Hound's Hill, the square in front of Central Station. Passengers on the toastrack might have caught a glimpse of a Marton car reversing there at the end of its journey from Talbot Square, and beyond it a little blue open-topper loading for the long run through the sandhills to Lytham.

From Central Station the driver took the toastrack cautiously along Central Beach – the "Golden Mile" as it was rather inaccurately known. When the tide

The first part of the Circular Tour was downhill from North Pier to Central Beach. Even Blackpool wasn't usually quite so crowded. This picture was taken from a southbound tram at the end of the Coronation celebrations in Talbot Square on 22 June 1911. A decorated Motherwell car is standing outside North Pier as sister car 42 arrives on the shuttle service from Victoria Pier. Just ahead of No. 42 is the crossover which clockwise Circulars used in the early years to reach Talbot Square. *(W.R. Buckley & Son)*

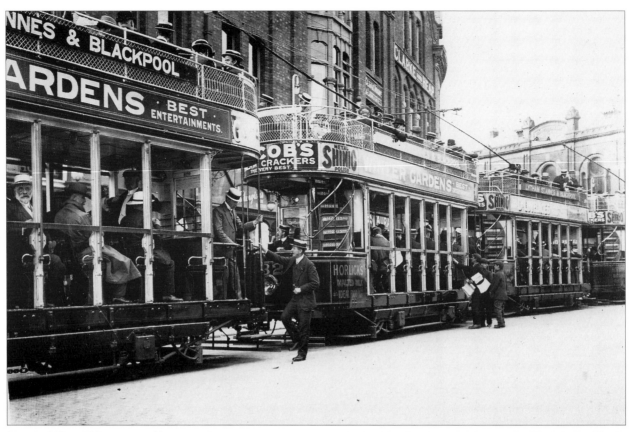

Hounds Hill on 12 June 1913 with a row of Lytham crossbench cars on the track leading from the Promenade. The Palatine Hotel is on the left, Feldman's Theatre on the right and Central Station behind the camera. Trams didn't normally load here, but this is a special occasion – delegates to the Tramways & Light Railway Congress taking a ride with their ladies to Lytham. *(DG)*

was in, the Promenade here would be packed with visitors, not all of them entirely alert to approaching trams. Despite the crowds, the accident rate was remarkably low – an average of three fatal accidents every two years.

One of the reasons for the large number of pedestrians around the Promenade tram track – and perhaps for the popularity of the Circular Tour - was that there were very few places to sit down. Blackpool didn't introduce deck chairs until Whitsuntide 1914, when 2,000 were hired at 2d. a day. Fifty were washed away on the first day, but within a month there were 4,600, and the traders on the sands were complaining about losing business.

The crowds were thickest near Central Pier, but thinned out a little by the Foxhall Hotel, where another single tram track crossed the road and disappeared mysteriously down a narrow street of terraced houses to the main tram depot in Blundell Street. By 1913 this was the last surviving section of the original conduit track of 1885; it was (and still is) the oldest electric street tramway in the world.

Manchester Square

Manchester Square, just south of the Foxhall, was the busiest junction on the system; until 1905 it had been the only

working junction on the whole of the Fylde tramways. The Lytham Road service turned off the Promenade here, as did the Circular itself before 1911. Manchester Square was also a summer terminus for the Lytham cars, and there would probably be a blue open-sided double-decker outside the Manchester Hotel.

Once past the Manchester, the toastrack driver could get the controller handle round on the long straight run past the boarding houses of South Promenade to Victoria Pier. On the way the toastrack might have passed the illuminated De Luxe car No. 68, still carrying its special message for the Royal Visit, "Long Life to our King and Queen", plus its normal all-purpose "Welcome to our Visitors" on the other side. No. 68 was only recently back from a rare visit to Lytham on 11 July.

Station Road

At Victoria Pier, Circular Tour passengers would see a line of trams ahead waiting to reverse on the four-track layout in front of the new Casino building which had opened at the Pleasure Beach only the week before the Bank Holiday. The toastrack avoided the queue by turning left into Station Road, a relatively minor street which carried tram traffic out of all proportion to its importance as a

thoroughfare. The west end of Station Road was the terminus for the Lytham Road route, as well as for another summer service of blue Lytham cars.

Diversion

The eastern end of Station Road was much busier in 1913 than it is today, with the Coast Line railway station still occupying its original position opposite the Grand Hotel (the entrance moved to Waterloo Road in May 1916). Here the blue cars turned right and the Lytham Road and Circular cars turned left. Except on one occasion which Harry Simpson, an old tram guard, recalled in 1967:

"I'll never forget the first time I guarded a Circular. George Mallett was driving and we set off from Talbot Square in fine style, turned off the Promenade at Victoria Pier and down Station Road.

"The junction at Lytham Road was a triangle in those days, and we turned smartly right, over the bridge, and were well on the way to Squires Gate before it struck me that something was up. 'George,' I said, 'we're going the wrong way.' 'By God, we are!' said George.

"Well, there wasn't much we could do about it by then. We had to carry on down to the next crossover, Highfield Road, turn round, and set off back to the Royal Oak. The only snag was that we

Above: The oldest electric trams in the world travelling along the oldest electric street tramway in Princess Street on a sombre occasion. Alexander Hollas, a fitter at the tram depot in Blundell Street, who lived nearby, died after falling into an inspection pit. On 5 January 1912 his coffin was borne from the depot at walking pace by conduit car 5, its warning bell draped in black, followed by No. 6 for the family and two Motherwell cars carrying mourners from the Tramway Department. The cortège took nearly 45 minutes to reach Layton Cemetery.

It was here in Princess Street that the first trials with electric traction took place on 2 July 1885, and this was also the last stretch of the old centre conduit to remain in place. At the 1913 Tramways & Light Railway Congress in Blackpool, the company who had supplied the original track suggested that this length of conduit be preserved, but nothing came of the idea and it was lifted around 1924. Happily the running rails are still there as an emergency route to the tram depot.

Below: During the height of the season a "step-lifter" was employed at the four-track Pleasure Beach terminus to raise and lower the steps of the trams – particularly heavy work on the double-staircase Dreadnoughts. This line-up consists of Lancaster car 13, Dreadnoughts 24 and (probably) 17, plus a four-wheeled Marton Box car which wouldn't do much to speed up loading, though the inspector doesn't seem unduly concerned. *(AMM)*

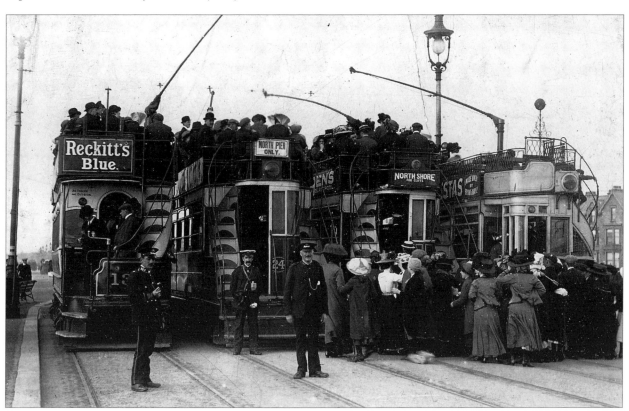

There was more to running Blackpool's trams than carrying cheerful holiday-makers round the Circular Tour in the sunshine. Marton Box cars 30 and 34 at Manchester Square on the afternoon of Sunday 5 November 1911, during the worst storm for ten years, with winds reaching 73 miles per hour.

couldn't for shame ask sixty-nine passengers to get off and stand in the road while we turned all the seats round. So there we were, running up Lytham Road with a tram-load of passengers all facing backwards.

"In the end we drove up Waterloo Road, turned left into Central Drive and reversed again at Bloomfield Road. By the time we got back to Talbot Square, the passengers had ridden over most of the tram track in Blackpool."

Harry and George can't have been too popular with the inspector at Talbot Square when they re-appeared hopelessly out of sequence. They would have been even less popular if they had gone the wrong way on that August weekend in

1913, but since there were forty trams running on the Tour during the Sunday afternoon, they could just have followed the one in front - on average it would only have been about 300 yards ahead of them.

Lytham Road

Assuming that the Circular Tour toastrack went left at the end of Station Road, it ran northwards for about 500 yards up Lytham Road. This was the main highway from St. Annes and Lytham, and at times the road and tram traffic rivalled that on the Promenade.

The Lytham cars came into town this way, but then - like the Circular - turned right at the Royal Oak into Waterloo

Road. Royal Oak was later the terminus for the Marton cars, but in 1913 it was simply a junction; there wasn't even a crossover for cars to reverse.

Waterloo Road

As soon as the toastrack turned into Waterloo Road, the driver had to put on full power - probably for the first time - to surmount the bridge over the Coast Line railway. Toastrack passengers wouldn't be able to see over the bridge, but those riding on top of a double-decker would have seen row upon row of railway carriages, of all shapes, sizes, colours and degrees of decrepitude, lined up in the massive carriage sidings which stretched out to the north of the bridge. As well as this array of custom-built sidings, every other obscure piece of track between Blackpool and Preston would be pressed into service to stable the excursion trains during the day.

From the railway bridge the driver could coast down to the Waterloo Hotel, where the toastrack might meet one of the Marton cars coming south from Central Station. It's not clear whether service cars had precedence over Circulars or vice versa. It probably didn't matter since agile residents would get on the toastrack anyway if there was room.

The Waterloo Hotel marked something of a change from the new South Shore to the old scattered community of Marton. The whole area had been common land until it was enclosed in 1767, and divided into the rectangular portions which gave the roads and eventually the tram routes of South Shore their distinctive grid pattern.

Once east of the Waterloo, there was a growing sense of being out in the sticks, as the houses thinned out and the

This is the junction of Lytham Road and Station Road, where Harry Simpson's toastrack turned right instead of left. Marton Box car 32 on the Lytham Road service is about to turn into Station Road outside the old South Shore railway station, which closed in 1916. The bridge over the Coast Line railway opened in May 1907, replacing the original skew bridge. The new bridge was built with some difficulty, as there was no firm foundation for 30 feet beneath the peat and silt.

line began to run between open fields. Waterloo Road - "Cow Gap Lane" until the trams arrived - ran straight and flat over the old common until it crossed the ancient route to Lytham at Spen Corner. There the tracks veered left and started to climb gradually to the Oxford Hotel.

Whitegate Drive

At the Oxford, the Circular turned left into Whitegate Drive. The Marton route became busier now, as there was an extra summer service of "turnback" cars running every ten minutes between the Oxford and Talbot Square. In the old days there had been a hill between the Oxford and the next small cluster of houses around the Saddle Inn, but it had been removed when the tramway was built in 1901.

Just past the Saddle, the tram depot loomed large - and a trifle incongruous - above the surrounding shops and houses. At quieter times, if the shed doors were open, Circular Tour passengers might glimpse rows of silent toastracks awaiting their call, but on this Bank Holiday weekend the depot would be empty, save perhaps for an old works car lurking unattended at the back of the shed whilst the engineering staff were busy driving trams.

Just beyond Marton Depot was the most attractive section of the Circular route as the line meandered along Whitegate Drive, sometimes described as Blackpool's only boulevard, being sufficiently far from the sea for trees to survive. This was where Charles Furness had organised his photo-session when the toastracks were new.

It was also where the well-to-do of Blackpool lived, and expensive villas dotted both sides of the road. But there were still open fields behind, and from

Throughout its long life, the Circular was operated from Marton Depot. Here, probably in 1911, the depot inspector watches Motherwell 46 being "trolleyed" into the shed after a day on the Tour; in those days the wires for the right-hand tracks were not connected to the rest of the overhead. On the left another Circular Tour Motherwell arrives home.

the higher ground to the west of Whitegate Drive it was possible to watch a Marton car leave the built-up area on Central Drive, and follow its progress for much of the way round the route.

There was another crossover outside Victoria Hospital (the old hospital, that is) which was sometimes used for short-workings from Talbot Square, though later the workings became shorter still and turned at Palatine Road instead.

Back into Town

Whitegate Drive ended at Devonshire Square, where the toastracks turned left past an attractive rustic tram shelter, and into Raikes Road. By now terraced houses were closing in again, and as Raikes Road narrowed to become Church Street, the toastrack ground to a halt. From here to Talbot Square, the

route was single-track, and at busy times a string of Circular Tour trams, plus a service car every five minutes, would be waiting for eastbound Marton cars to clear the line.

At one point during that weekend in 1913, eleven Circular Tour cars were queuing to get through the single track. They spent longer fighting their way through the four passing loops between Raikes Road and Talbot Square than they had taken to travel from Talbot Square to Raikes Road.

By now the passengers would be fidgeting; there were better things to do in Blackpool on a hot Bank Holiday weekend than sit in a queue of trams. Before long they would start climbing down and heading for the Promenade or wherever. By the time the tram reached Talbot Square - often after a trip lasting

In August 1911 top-covered Marton Box car 35 briefly disturbs the tranquillity of Whitegate Drive on its way from Central Station to Talbot Square. Blackpool's uncertain sub-soil is proving inadequate to anchor the pole on the left against the pull of the heavy copper wire round the reverse curve. *(R.W. Lord/PJ)*

Above: Toastrack 78 waits in the loop outside the Winter Gardens in August 1913, with the Big Wheel towering 200 feet into the sky behind. The tram driver is relaxing against the nearside step but most of his passengers have tired of waiting.

Below: Another impatient passenger leaves the Circular Tour in August 1913, as De Luxe car 65 appears round the corner from Clifton Street and the toastrack can at last move on to the next passing loop. Originally the single track was controlled by a boy waving a red or white flag, but in 1904 the light halfway up the pole on the left was installed, operated automatically by the "skate" on the wire in front of the toastrack. By 1920 the boy with the flags was back – different boy, but same flags apparently. After the *Blackpool Times* complained that he seemed to be waving his month-old handkerchief, he was given brand-new flags in red and green. Boy and flags both became redundant when the road was widened and the track doubled in 1926. *(Edward Sankey)*

an hour instead of the normal forty minutes – it would be nearly empty. But not for long. That weekend the crowds were still waiting in the Square even after it had gone dark.

Too Good to Last

At the end of that August Bank Holiday the day trippers and the weekenders finally set off for home, tired but content and not a little inebriated. It was half past midnight before the last excursion left Talbot Road Station for its long journey through the night to South Wales.

It had been a weekend of superlatives. Never before had so many postcards been posted, so many children lost, so many passengers carried on the Circular Tour. It was the high point of Blackpool's Edwardian heyday.

Some of those sleepy passengers who had bought a newspaper to read on the train might have noticed a paragraph headed "Outrages in the Balkans". It must have seemed a million miles away. But twelve months later, outrages in the Balkans would change their world for ever. And many of those young men who had escorted their elegant ladies so proudly round Blackpool on the toastracks during that wonderful weekend in 1913, would never ride the Circular Tour again.

Above: **At the end of another long day on the Circular Tour in 1913, the toastracks are gradually reverting to Promenade duties. Here in Talbot Square car 71 has changed its destination boards to "Promenade" and its blind to "South Shore". Some of No. 71's Tour passengers have stayed on to ride back to their lodgings, while the toastrack behind has picked up a few more passengers for another trip round the Circular.**

Below: **The red crosses on De Luxe car 66 and Dreadnought 61 are publicising Hospital Saturday, an annual fund-raising event for Victoria Hospital. But they could just as well be symbolising the end of an era for the hundreds of holiday-makers in this poignant view of the Pleasure Beach terminus on 1 August 1914; three days later the country was at war.** *(William P. Beck)*

Flag-Waving and Fund-Raising

Above: The wartime recruiting authorities found Blackpool a particularly hard nut to crack: at a rally in Warbreck Road Drill Hall in November 1914, not a single person turned up. On 6 March 1915 they organised this recruitment parade in Talbot Square, and the Tramways Department provided a decorated tram – four-wheel De Luxe car No. 62. This is the only known photograph of No. 62 with the experimental windscreens which had been fitted in December 1912.

Below: On 17 February 1918 Blackpool received a surplus tank as the focus of its "Tank Week" fund-raising. Numbered 113 and named "Julian", the tank had already seen similar service in London, Manchester, Edinburgh, Dundee and Glasgow. The Mayor of Blackpool, Albert Lindsay Parkinson launched Tank Week from the top of Julian outside the Town Hall in Talbot Square *(left)*. Five months later Lindsay Parkinson made a more significant contribution to the history of Blackpool, when he personally bought the Fleetwood Tramroad for £260,000 and passed it over to the Corporation for the same amount. *(R.W. Lord)*

To swell the Tank Week coffers, it was decided to mount a surprise assault on the affluent residents of Lytham. Julian's mobility being somewhat limited – its brief journey from the railway goods yard to the Town Hall played havoc with the surface of Talbot Road – the Tramways Department had built a travelling replica on the remains of an old conduit car. It was named "Albert" after the Mayor and carried his telephone number, 88. On 20 February Albert entered Lytham, guns blazing and led by a band from the military hospital at Squires Gate. The tank advanced as far as Bannister Street on the Cottage Hospital route, possibly the furthest point a Blackpool tram ever reached in Lytham. It then made a tactical withdrawal to the town centre, where it spent the rest of the day on the little-used tracks in Clifton Square *(right)*, selling tickets for the Electricity & Tramways Department Prize Draw. *(TS)*

3. The Circular Tour : War and Peace

TALBOT SQUARE BLACKPOOL

During the summer of 1914 the Circular Tour looked certain to surpass even 1913's remarkable performance. By July, when yet another batch of six new toastracks went into service, takings were up by 15%. Business was phenomenal; at one point during the August Bank Holiday, seven toastracks were queuing up to clear the crowds in Talbot Square.

Perhaps people realised that things were about to change. Throughout the week of the Bank Holiday – in those days, the first Monday in August – the town was crowded with visitors. But events were increasingly over-shadowed by news from Europe. Visitors still rode the Circular Tour, though all around them were signs of growing tension. Armed soldiers suddenly appeared outside the railway stations. Then all the German and Austrian catering staff headed for home, leaving the Cleveleys Hydro with three cooks instead of ten for five hundred guests.

Wartime

War was declared on Tuesday 4 August. The London & North Western Railway immediately cancelled all their excursion trains and the Lancashire & Yorkshire most of theirs, leaving visitors queuing for hours at the stations to get home on the Saturday. Only 28 excursions arrived the following Saturday, and the expected record season was in serious trouble.

In an attempt to salvage the situation, the Corporation pressed on with the

By 1914 the Corporation were becoming increasingly concerned at the growing motor traffic on the Promenade and introduced several measures to control it. The bollard and island on the right were highly controversial when they were installed in December 1913. On the left the original sleeping policeman waits to stop the traffic for new toastrack No. 91 to cross from Talbot Square onto the Promenade.

Autumn Illuminations despite much local controversy and a communiqué from the Admiralty requesting municipal authorities "to reduce as much as possible the number of powerful electric lights on piers, esplanades and public places which are visible from the sea or from the air".

The season did, in fact, recover quite well, though by the end of the year the number of Circular Tour passengers had fallen below not just 1913's but 1912's

figure as well. However Blackpool quickly bounced back from the initial shock of the war, and tram traffic started to soar in 1915. Affluent workers in the textile and munitions industries still came for days out, and the town was full of troops training or convalescing.

At Whitsuntide 1915, the *Blackpool Times* remarked that "the tram traffic in Church Street has been abnormal; there appears to be a greater number of

The declaration of war on 4 August came right at the height of the 1914 season, and spoiled what would have been a record year for the Circular Tour. Business looks pretty slow for toastrack 85 as it waits on the siding outside North Pier with just one passenger on board, and another empty toastrack behind. The time is around one o'clock, so perhaps it's the lunchtime lull.

Tours of Duty, 1914 – 1918

Above: In October 1914, 54 wounded Belgian soldiers – a great novelty at the time – arrived at Victoria Hospital on Whitegate Drive. Most were only light casualties and were judged well enough to be taken by toastrack No. 78 for a three-hour tour of the town on 17 October. Crowds gathered outside the Hospital to see them off. Women spectators cut buttons off the soldiers' uniforms as souvenirs; one gave the victim half-a-crown in return, and the tour soon turned into an impromptu fund-raising exercise. Altogether £86 was raised in a fervour of support for "gallant little Belgium". The toastrack ran to Talbot Square, Gynn, Victoria Pier, then via Lytham Road to Central Station, where it crossed into Hounds Hill and returned to the Hospital via Central Drive. *(BL)*

Below: Before very long, wounded soldiers were anything but a novelty in Blackpool: altogether 37,620 of them passed through the military hospital at Squires Gate. Wounded or not, this group have had to dismount and turn their seats as photographer Lord follows his usual face-the-light routine on Whitegate Drive. The date must be 1917 or 1918, after the Corporation recruited women as tram drivers. *(R.W. Lord)*

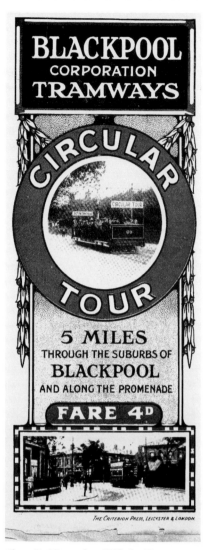

toastracks and large-sized tramcars using the street than ever before." The reference to "large-sized" cars is intriguing, since this was usually how the Dreadnoughts were described. However there is no evidence that Dreadnoughts were ever used on the Circular; their top-deck capacity would have been useful, but their end-loading arrangements would have been even more lethal in the busy town centre than they were on the Promenade.

As more and more men went into the Army, the Corporation recruited women as conductors in June 1915 and drivers in March 1917. The toastracks were unpopular with women conductors because of the difficulties of collecting fares from the running boards, but were frequently allocated to women drivers, who found them easier to brake than the heavy double-deckers.

Postwar Problems

During the war, passenger figures for the Circular remained remarkably level at around 500,000 a year. Although the Tour never again managed to regain the heights of the 1913 season, the first postwar summer of 1919 came very close. The railway companies had reduced excursions drastically from their pre-war level, but motor charabancs made up the shortfall. One newspaper was struck by how much more colourful the toastrack passengers suddenly were after the sombre fashions which had prevailed during the war - the women in vivid greens and oranges, and the men in bright shirts and ties instead of khaki.

1919 also saw one of the most remarkable days in the life of the Circular Tour. On Saturday 21 June – the longest

Above: In November 1913 the Tramways Department ordered 100,000 of these folding maps of the Circular Tour route. The map itself appears on the back cover of this book.

Above: **Women conductors found their long skirts ill-suited to collecting fares from the running-boards of toastracks. Agnes Park had joined the Tramways Department in March 1916. Her father, Charlie Park, was permanent way foreman and had been with the tramway since conduit days. Agnes was employed on munitions work in the tram depot at Blundell Street, which during the war produced 150,000 shells. She only worked as a tram conductress during the Easter weekend, but thought it worth having her photograph taken.**

Below: **An unusual view of toastrack 69 turning into Station Road, carefully negotiating the points which led onto a short siding outside Victoria Pier. The year is probably 1921, as the toastracks have their new headlights but the street lamps have still not been re-fitted after the wartime blackout and postwar coal shortages. On the right the old South Shore vicarage is up for sale; the vicar had found it too large and moved to the Queen's Hydro. The building eventually became a café and later a gift shop.**

Getting on and off toastracks was never easy, but didn't need to be quite as difficult as the bowler-hatted gentleman is making it on No. 81 in this early Twenties view in Talbot Square. From the prosperous appearance of the passengers, this could well be a conference party.

day of the year – 100,000 Lancashire and Cheshire miners descended on Blackpool in 138 special trains for their Annual "Picnic". The first contingent arrived at two o'clock in the morning to be greeted by pouring rain, but by the time the Tower opened and the Circular Tour started running, the weather had brightened, and the day's festivities could begin. It was five o'clock. During the rest of that long, long day the Circular Tour carried 11,524 passengers – a record for a Saturday which would never be equalled.

So popular was the Circular in 1919 that at the height of the season it was taking almost as much money as the Promenade route. On the busiest day of all, Sunday 10 August, more than 250 trips were run and 18,731 passengers carried. Tour receipts for the year were an all-time record of £11,725, partly because the fare went up from 4d. to 6d. at Whit. In a period of postwar inflation, nobody seemed to mind.

1920 was almost as good as 1919, but then came a disastrous year in 1921,

when the Circular was dealt a double blow. First came a coal strike, which severely restricted tram services in general and stopped them altogether on Sundays. Then the Corporation began relaying the Lytham Road and Marton tracks, a job which should have been done during the war years. Normally this would have been a winter task, but the work was so urgent that it couldn't be delayed.

The Marton route had to be run in two parts, either side of the excavations, so running the Circular was out of the question. In the whole of the 1921 season, Tour receipts amounted to precisely £9.11.4½d. This came about through the unwitting involvement of the Prince of Wales, who visited Blackpool on 8 July and travelled out of town via Lytham Road. The roadworks there were hastily made good, and some enterprising tram inspector managed to sneak seven Circular Tours through before the tracks were dug up again.

When the relaying programme reached Central Drive in 1923, severely disrupting the Marton service, there was an interesting reversion to the early days of the Circular route. For a few weeks from 5 February the Marton cars, instead of turning right into Central Drive at the Waterloo Hotel, ran straight on to Royal Oak and back along Lytham Road to Talbot Square - just as the original Circular had done in 1905.

Decline

The Circular Tour resumed normal running in 1922, but during the missing year visitors seemed to have found other things to do, and the Tour never quite

Toastrack No. 80 on the Circular Tour at Devonshire Square follows No. 77 on its way to the Promenade. The combined shelter and sub-station was built in 1921 to replace a rustic shelter which was re-sited at Thornton railway station to serve the Corporation's first bus route.

Facing the Camera at the Oxford Hotel

From the end of the First World War, a group photograph on the toastrack outside the Oxford Hotel was part of the fun of the Circular Tour.

To be honest, few of those on board looked to be having much fun, and generally the tram crews seemed to be enjoying themselves more than the passengers. They probably were - driving a Circular Tour toastrack was pretty easy work, and guarding one easier still, once the fares were in.

The photographer was only there at busy times. The Oxford was part of a daily circuit which also covered the comings and goings of the morning and afternoon charabanc excursions.

Officially the Corporation frowned on the photograph and instructed tram drivers not to stop at the Oxford, but the photographer found that a regular distribution of cigarettes at the tram depot each Christmas produced a suitably Nelsonian approach to this edict.

Bill Latham, son of the Oxford Hotel's landlord, was one of the local children who were recruited to hold the exposure number on the toastrack's steps. The photographer then handed out numbered tickets for passengers to collect their prints next day at the Winter Gardens.

For this duty, Bill was paid a penny, which he immediately spent at Wilsons' sweet shop just round the corner. Since his normal pocket money was only 2d. a week, he was well pleased with the arrangement.

In July 1927 the Tramway Committee resolved that "the tram drivers and conductors are to be instructed to discontinue the practice of stopping Circular Tour tramcars for photographs to be taken" and this apparently had the desired effect.

By then the Tour was beginning to lose its appeal anyway, and the photographer seems to have found richer pickings on the Corporation's new runabout buses at Stanley Park.

Above: The Circular Tour photographer usually stood alongside the toastrack, so this view of No. 76, gleaming in its coach-painter's varnish, is one of the few Oxford Hotel pictures to show the number of the tram. The year is probably 1921, when the toastracks were fitted with headlights and had their dash panels (at least) repainted. The photographer's assistant is setting up the number of the picture, a task usually sub-contracted to local children for a penny a session.

Below: Bill Latham, aged about seven, earns his morning penny outside the laburnum-shrouded Oxford Hotel, where his father was landlord. This picture was taken not long before the Corporation stopped the Circular Tour photographs in 1927.

In June 1923, the Corporation organised a Carnival on the lines of the one held at Nice. Flags and festoons were hung in all the main streets, and along the fairy lights of the toastrack trams. This is No. 76 turning from Abingdon Street into Clifton Street late one afternoon. A second Carnival in 1924 got rather out of hand, and the Corporation restored the Illuminations instead in 1925.

recovered its popularity. Passenger figures hovered around the 300,000 mark for a few years, up or down a little according to the weather. Then, after a brief peak of 350,000 passengers during the fine summer of 1925, toastrack riding began to fall alarmingly.

In a way, this was inevitable. It was a time of new attractions in Blackpool - motor coach trips, aeroplane joy-rides, and large new features on the Pleasure Beach, besides expensive municipal attractions such as Stanley Park and the huge open-air baths at South Shore. In 1928 passengers fell below 200,000 for the first time since Charles Furness re-launched the Tour in 1911. By 1930 they were down to 100,000 and the Circular Tour looked to be in terminal decline.

But in the same way as Charles Furness had revived the Circular's flagging fortunes after John Lancaster's death in 1910, so a new protagonist appeared. William Campbell was appointed Traffic Superintendent in November 1929, primarily because the Committee wanted someone with experience of buses.

Despite his bus credentials, Campbell soon emerged as a champion of the Circular Tour - like most traffic men, he was probably captivated by the sheer profitability of the operation, even with only 100,000 passengers a year. He set about extending the Circular along New South Promenade to Squires Gate and back via Lytham Road.

The idea had been around for a long time but didn't seem to be getting very far. The Tramways Department had first proposed it as long ago as 1912, but because of the war and protracted negotiations for the purchase of the land along the shore, it was 1926 before the new tracks along New South Promenade opened, and 1932 before the Circular Tour itself was extended.

The old route via Station Road, which had begun so spectacularly in 1911, ended dismally in March 1932. Easter was early that year and the weather was poor. On Good Friday only one trip was made, and none at all on the Saturday. On Easter Sunday, 27 March, there were four runs, which only carried 135 passengers. The weather was better on Easter Monday, but for some reason the Circular didn't run at all. The old route just faded away.

By the late Twenties the Circular Tour cars no longer had things all their own way on the streets of Blackpool. Near Palatine Road, toastrack 75 is having to share Whitegate Drive with a 1925 Riley, a Model T Ford, a Ribble bus and an assortment of school-children. The green tram stop signs, derived from the Circular Tour device, lasted until the Sixties. *(BTD)*

Tramcar tourists besiege one of the Fleetwood Tramroad's "Vanguard" cars, as the conductor prepares to turn the trolley at the terminus outside Talbot Road railway station on Thursday 10 August 1916. Wartime pressures - too many passengers and too few tram drivers – affected the Fleetwood Tramroad just as much as the Corporation. Visitors had taken to walking down Dickson Road, boarding an inbound tram (at a penny fare) and then sitting tight at the terminus, which can't have gone down too well with the crowds waiting there. Orderly queues like this were a new phenomenon, born of patient waiting for rationed wartime supplies; before then queueing had been regarded as a rather effete Continental habit. There may have been a sadder reason for this particular delay, as there was a fatal accident on the Tramroad at Fleetwood that day.

*O*f the Fylde's three tramway systems, the one that relied most on tourist traffic - at least in its early days - was the Blackpool & Fleetwood Tramroad. So it's perhaps fitting that the Tramroad had a tour which started before the Corporation's Circular Tour, finished later and covered - on and off - a period of 82 years.

To be fair, the Pilling Tour was off much more than it was on, and carried fewer passengers in its entire life than the Circular Tour did in one weekend during 1913. But it has an interesting history, not least because it involved several different forms of transport.

Pilling is a small village "Over Wyre" as they say, and - like St. Michael's - the right distance from Blackpool to appeal to charabanc operators. And just as charabancs were one of the reasons for introducing the Corporation's Tour, so they provoked a similar response from the Blackpool & Fleetwood Tramroad.

The Tramroad Company

The Tramroad had been created by a powerful alliance of local landowners with major engineering and electrical companies, financed by Manchester and Scottish capitalists and presided over by some of the most experienced tramway entrepreneurs in the country. It was built on the American style, with long single-deck bogie cars running across country on private tracks – even its title sounded vaguely transatlantic, though "tramroad" was an ancient term, more often applied to mineral railways. The line opened between Fleetwood and the Gynn on 14 July 1898, and along Warbreck Road and Dickson Road to Talbot Road railway station two months later.

The Tramroad's immediate success surprised even its most optimistic supporters. In the first full year of operation, the Company made a profit of £10,000 on income of £30,000. In 1902, however, receipts fell for the first time, though only from £30,958 to £30,527. Charabanc competition was identified as one of the reasons, and the Tramroad Company decided that it was time to play the Blackpool livery stables at their own game.

A Toe in the Water

The Tramroad Company were already involved in the charabanc business by the back door. Since July 1901 they had been participating in a Circular Tour organised by the brewers Magee Marshall and operated by Hill & Tillotson, a long-established livery stable in Blackpool.

The charabanc left the Clarence Hotel outside Central Station at 10.30 each morning, and ran via Poulton and Shard Bridge across the River Wyre to Knott

Above: **The charabanc Circular Tour to Knott End started outside the Clarence Hotel in Hound's Hill. Here a row of charabancs and wagonettes are ready for the off. Charabancs had forward-facing seats, often raked up to the back. Wagonettes were smaller and the passengers faced each other.**

Below: **The Queen Street & Dickson Road Livery Stables were already advertising wagonette drives when this early photograph was taken at Talbot Road, probably in 1899. Loading a Fleetwood Box car was an inefficient process, even when the passengers had no luggage.**

End, arriving at about 12.30. Passengers could re-cross the river by ferry to Fleetwood and catch the tram back to Blackpool, or return later in the afternoon on the charabanc.

A Ride on the Pilling Tour

On 3 August 1903 the Tramroad Company launched their own tour to Pilling and Garstang. This was no brief excursion, but a proper day out. Passengers doing the full journey had to leave Blackpool before 10.30 to be back the same day.

It would be nice to say that the

Tramroad's enterprise in organising this marathon excursion was well rewarded, but it wasn't; before the First World War, receipts never reached £100 a year. However the Pilling Tour became a sort of icon for the Tramroad - something they felt they ought to keep going. And years later, after the Corporation took over the Tramroad Company, the Tour enjoyed an unexpected heyday in the Twenties, and a series of revivals right down to the 1980s.

The Tour started at the Tramroad's terminus in the street outside Talbot Road railway station. Tour passengers could board any of the Company's trams: closed "Box" saloons, or open-sided crossbench cars, some (known as "Yankees") with an unusual arrangement of sideways-facing seats at each end, to avoid having steps over the bogies.

The first stretch of the Tour was hardly scenic, along Dickson Road and Warbreck Road, where the most prominent sights were the backs of the boarding houses on the sea-front. From time to time Tour passengers would glimpse the Corporation's Dreadnought cars running along the Promenade to the Gynn, and perhaps wonder why the Tramroad cars didn't go that way. So did the Tramroad Company, but it's a

complicated story and this isn't really the place to tell it.

The Dickson Road Bottleneck

Progress along this single-track section of the route was fitful at best. The line as far as the boundary just north of the Gynn had been built by the Corporation and leased to the Company, and was a perpetual bone of contention.

The problems were at their worst on summer Saturdays, when the Fleetwood cars were crowded with holiday-makers going to and from the railway station. The closed Box cars were desperately slow-loading, particularly for passengers with luggage. Before fixed stops were introduced in 1903, a Saturday journey along Dickson Road would be punctuated by long waits at street corners as visitors arrived near their lodgings.

Speed Trap

To make up for the delays, the Tramroad drivers scuttled along the single track from loop to loop as fast as they could, but once more fell foul of the Corporation. The Tramroad's Parliamentary Act had laid down a maximum speed of eight miles per hour through the streets, and the Corporation were determined to enforce it.

Matters came to a head in August 1899 when Blackpool's Chief Constable organised a sort of Victorian speed trap. Two policemen with stop watches were stationed 235 yards apart at Derby Road and Warley Road (235 yards would take exactly a minute at eight m.p.h.).

The trap netted four victims before, presumably, word got around. The drivers of crossbench cars 1, 3 and 5 and Box car 22 were fined varying amounts for "furious driving". The course record and the highest fine of £1 or 28 days' hard labour went to driver John Pilling on car 5 with a time of 39 seconds, which worked out at 12.4 m.p.h.

The Gynn

At Warley Road the line curved down a 1-in-26 gradient, the steepest on the line, to the Gynn Inn. This stretch of track was laid as "double-single" - two tracks laid closely together so that trams could pass parked vehicles, but couldn't pass each other.

At the Gynn, Pilling Tourists got their first real view of the sea. Then the car turned onto a short paved reservation to climb a 1-in-42 hill to the boundary. The Company had wanted this section to be laid as sleeper track, but the Corporation insisted on grooved rail, expensive wooden setts and ornamental centre poles.

Originally the Gynn had been a deep defile in the cliffs, so deep that the initial

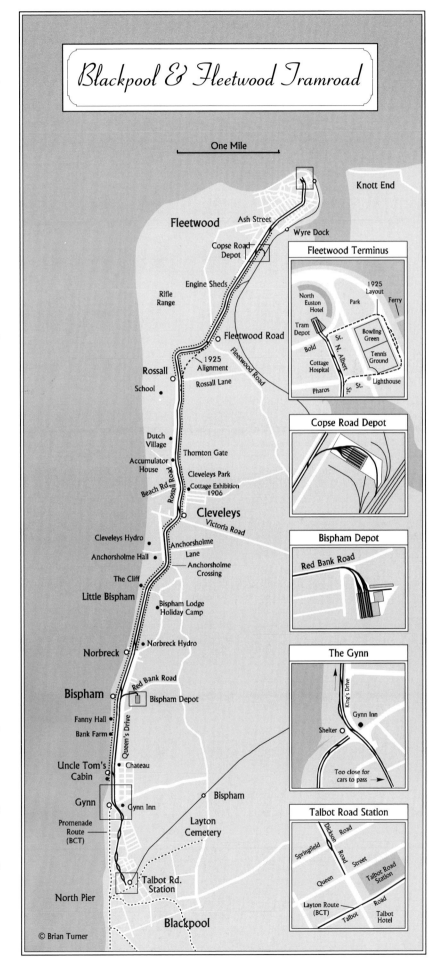

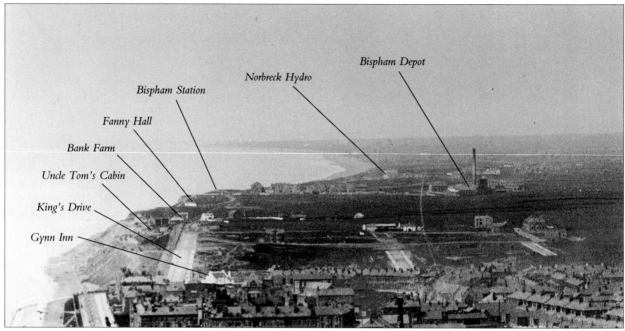

The landscape of the Fleetwood Tramroad, seen from the top of Blackpool Tower around 1901, showing King's Drive laid out as far as Uncle Tom's Cabin.

plans for the Tramroad had allowed for a bridge across to the northern side. The cliffs there were partly lowered in 1896, just before the Tramroad was built, saving the expense of the bridge. Even so the land near the boundary was still high enough for the new Tramroad to run through a cutting, with a wooden footbridge over it, before the cliffs were brought down closer to track level in 1899.

Uncle Tom's Cabin

Once across the boundary into Bispham, the Tramroad quickly threw off its municipal pretensions and began to look very much the serious railway. The poles lost their ornamentation and the line became open sleeper track, protected by

cattle grids and a metal fence.

Just north of the boundary, on the seaward side of the line, stood Uncle Tom's Cabin, which had been Blackpool's first regular place of amusement in 1857. The land on the west of the line became quite a lively spot with stalls and entertainers, though the gipsies who had lived near the Cabin for years had moved to South Shore.

The coming of the Tramroad helped restore the Cabin's fading fortunes for a while, but could do nothing for its perilous perch on the cliffs. The Tramroad Company had worries enough of its own, as the accelerating erosion began to threaten the line itself. Between 1890 and 1910, the cliffs eroded by 100 feet and in some places were less than

that distance from the Tramroad.

It was to be many years before the cliff-edge was eventually (and expensively) stabilised by the Corporation after they had absorbed Bispham into the borough in 1918 - much too late for Uncle Tom's Cabin, which was pulled down at the end of 1907 and replaced by a new public house on the east side of the road.

In true railway style, the Tramroad Company built substantial brick stations at their major stops, with waiting-rooms and lavatories, and station-masters in charge. For some reason the station at the Cabin wasn't built until May 1903, when a half-timbered building, quite different from the normal style, was erected on the west of the line just south of the Cabin.

The Gynn could be a bleak spot at times. The wind is whistling across from the Corporation tram terminus just off to the right, as Box car 24 circumnavigates the Gynn Inn and heads for Warbreck Road. The date is around 1901.

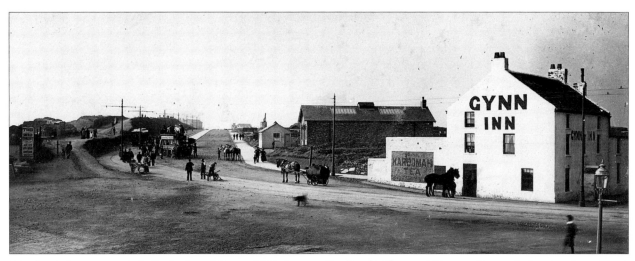

An animated panorama at the beginning of August 1898, three weeks after the Fleetwood Tramroad opened. Crossbench car No. 4 is taking passengers from the bus *Ethel*, which is being given a new three-horse team from the stables at the Gynn Inn. The building behind the inn is the Tramroad's accumulator house. The road alongside the tramway ran only as far as the Blackpool boundary at the top of the hill. It was extended to the Cabin in 1899 and to Norbreck in 1904. A small gang of men with a tar-boiler are working on the extension to Talbot Road, which the Tramroad – much to the Corporation's annoyance – declined to open on the grounds that they didn't have enough trams. *(BL)*

The *Blackpool Times* described it as "a neat Olde Englyshe station - white, with green cross-beams and warm red-tiled roof."

At 94 feet above sea level, the Cabin was the highest point on the coast for many miles in each direction. On a good day, Pilling Tourists could make out the Isle of Man sixty miles away. Those of a romantic disposition would probably be more interested in an unusual building just north of the Cabin. It had been built in 1906 by Arthur Knowles after the style of a chateau to suit his new French wife, who visited it twice and decided to stay

in France. The chateau remained empty almost continually until 1935, when it was sold for £14,500, and became the Blackpool home of the famous music publisher Lawrence Wright. It is now a casino.

Along the Cliff Top

The empty chateau was one of the few properties on the sea-front between the Cabin and Bispham. The Gynn Estate Company, who owned the land from the Gynn to Bispham and were in close cahoots with the Tramroad Company, claimed to have staked out new roads for

seaside villas along this length. But most of the houses they sold in the early years were cheaper terraced properties further inland, away from the crumbling coast.

In fact there were almost as many buildings on the west of the Tramroad as on the east. Just north of the Cabin a pierrot group called the Empire Serenaders performed several times a day in a small open-air pavilion near the present St. Stephen's Avenue. A footpath across the Tramroad there was known for years afterwards as Serenaders' Crossing.

With the coastline receding by as much as five feet a year, it's clear that at

The fortune-tellers and amusements remained on the cliffs after the old Cabin was demolished at the end of 1907. When this picture of crossbench car 26 standing at Cabin station was taken in 1915, Arthur Knowles's deserted "chateau" across the road was being used to house Belgian refugees.

Above: Box car 22 leaves the last of the amusements behind and heads off along the cliffs to Bispham. The buildings of Bank Farm are still standing on the west of the tram track, but Fanny Hall has gone, which suggests a date around 1909. The Camera Obscura on the right once stood on the cliff-edge near Uncle Tom's Cabin.

Below: By the time this photograph was taken on the Bispham cliffs in May 1913, Pilling Tourists would have looked in vain for Bank Farm. In its place was this precarious *al fresco* reading-room, with novels, magazines and deck chairs each costing 2d. Deck chairs were quite a novelty at the time; Blackpool itself didn't allow them until 1914. It seems that when patrons finished reading their magazines – novels perhaps took longer - they disposed of them over the cliff. These days nobody would be allowed within a hundred yards of the place. *(R.W. Lord)*

one time the farms and cottages must have extended well to the west of the site of the Tramroad. There were still two relics of this old settlement, which the Bispham parish registers referred to as "Blackpool Bank".

The first was Bank Farm, which the Tramroad neatly bisected, leaving the farmhouse on the east of the line and the outbuildings on the west; in January 1904 the Company had to pay the farmer £92 after a tram killed some of his cows. The farm was demolished around 1910. The other old building was a cottage with the curious name of Fanny Hall, opposite what is now the Miners' Home tram stop; it disappeared around 1907.

Bispham

Bispham was the headquarters of the Tramroad Company, and contained its main depot and offices as well as houses for most of its regular staff. The Tramroad was rapidly transforming Bispham. The population, around 500 for decades, doubled between 1891 and 1901 and had reached 1,500 by the time the Pilling Tour started in 1903.

Bispham tram station stood, like most of the others, on the west of the tracks. Opposite the station, a single track curved back from the south-bound line originally through fields in a cutting which led down to Bispham Depot, 300 yards away. The cutting was soon

The outbuildings of Bank Farm on the seaward side of the track, with King's Drive and the Tramroad in the foreground. (R.W. Lord)

opened out by the Norbreck Estate Company (like the Gynn Estate, closely connected with the founders of the Tramroad) to become Red Bank Road.

Norbreck

The stretch from Bispham to Norbreck was the fastest on the line – dead straight on a falling gradient. The cliffs along here were protected from erosion by a bank of shingle and had been stable for at least fifty years.

At Norbreck there was the usual brick station on the west of the line. Next to it the track crossed a lane which ran up from the beach, across the end of Queen's Drive and through Norbreck village. The main source of passenger traffic was the Hydropathic Hotel

opposite the tram station. The hotel had been gradually developed from the old Norbreck Villa by a Manchester businessman, from 1900 onwards.

Until 1932, Norbreck was the end of King's/Queen's Drive. The parallel road had been completed in 1904, but seems to have brought little competition for the trams. During one of the busiest days of Blackpool's best season in August 1913, the road was used by only 80 horse-drawn vehicles, 14 motor cars, three motor cycles and 150 pedal cycles between 7 a.m. and 5 p.m.

Beyond Norbreck the Tramroad ran alongside the grounds and tennis courts of the Hydro, straight and level to Little Bispham. To the east of the track was the Bispham Lodge Holiday Camp, which

Bispham Station has always been a good place to watch the trams. Box car 16 takes on passengers for Blackpool around 1913. The lane on the left was the original road from Bispham village to the sea, before the tram track to the depot was turned into Red Bank Road. (R.W. Lord)

which later became "Pat's Pantry" and was demolished in 1938 to make room for a new turning circle.

Ideally the Tramroad would have continued right along the seashore to Rossall and Fleetwood. But the coastline was occupied by two large properties – Anchorsholme Hall and Eryngo Lodge, both dating from the 1850s – and the line was forced inland. It was the last time Pilling Tourists would see the sea before they reached Fleetwood.

Anchorsholme

From Little Bispham the Tramroad ran down a shallow cutting to a sharp left curve which took it over the lane from Bispham village to Cleveleys at what is still called Anchorsholme Crossing. Then it followed the east side of the lane to a halt which served the Cleveleys Hydropathic Hotel. The Hydro, with its 25-acre grounds on the seafront, had been expanded from Eryngo Lodge and opened in July 1899. Like the Norbreck Hydro and the Bispham Lodge Holiday Camp, it had been developed to take advantage of the new Tramroad.

Just north of the Hydro the trams negotiated a sinuous reverse curve which took them across Victoria Road and into Cleveleys tram station.

Post by Tram

Until the Tramroad arrived, Cleveleys had been something of a backwater. Its links with the rest of the Coast were so

Above: **Crossbench car 25 at the top of Red Bank Road on the track leading down to Bispham Depot. Bispham Station can just be seen behind the car. The date is about 1905.**

Below: **Northbound passengers prepare to board Box car 14 as it sweeps down the race track from Bispham into a sandy Norbreck station, around 1914.**

was mainly a camping site for tents (21/– per week – men only) and was served by a halt between Norbreck and Little Bispham.

There was another halt at Little Bispham itself with a shelter, but no proper station building until 1935. Just north of the halt, to the west of the track, was a house called "The Cliff",

Box car 15 arrives at Cleveleys tram station from the south just before dusk. The car has picked up its oil headlamp at Bispham Station ready for the return journey. Victoria Road leads off to the right towards Thornton. *(AC)*

poor that letters to Blackpool were routed via Preston. In 1902 Cleveleys residents petitioned the Post Office for a mail service along the coast. On 1 October 1903 the petition bore fruit in the form of a large letter box "of ornate design" attached to the back of a southbound Tramroad car roughly every hour. Letters could be posted at any tram station. At Talbot Road a postman took the box to the GPO and the letters went out with the next post. In those days there were several deliveries a day, and a letter posted in Fleetwood at 4.45 p.m. would be delivered in Blackpool on the 5.30 round.

The new service was a great success. A Manchester newspaper reported that at Cleveleys, Norbreck and Bispham "there is quite a muster of visitors, children, maid-servants and others, all with letters and picture postcards ready to drop into the box. 'Waiting for the post' is almost one of the social events of the day." On several occasions the boxes were "jammed with missives", according to the *Blackpool Gazette*, and one night in December 1903, "on the arrival of the mail tram at Cleveleys, no less than eighteen people were waiting to post their letters."

The Tramroad Company were less impressed. Eighteen people were very welcome if they boarded the tram, but not when they milled round the back of the car, delaying it for the best part of a minute, and then disappeared into the night. So the Company had few regrets when the Post Office decided to provide proper letter boxes at the tram stations and send one of their new motor vans to

empty them four times a day. The last Tramroad postal car ran on 16 February 1908.

Thornton Gate and Rossall

The Tramroad between Cleveleys and Rossall lay on the landward side of Rossall Road, which provided a roundabout and poorly surfaced route from Cleveleys to Fleetwood. At Thornton Gate the cars passed a mysterious brick building on the left of the track. This was the "battery house", full of accumulators which were charged up from Bispham power station during the quieter hours, and then released to boost the inadequate supply at the Fleetwood end when traffic was heavy.

North of Thornton Gate, the land on the east of the line was still agricultural,

but to the west was the public school at Rossall. This was another significant source of traffic for the Tramroad Company, who also supplied the science laboratory with distilled water from the battery house at Thornton Gate. There was a brick station at Rossall, which still exists, though not in the same position.

Curiously the only stretch of cross-country track to survive today, between Rossall and Broadwater, is the one part of the route which isn't original. The current alignment was opened in 1925 to replace an awkward right-angle bend where the original line followed the old flood banks across this low-lying land. The route was changed to make room for the new main road from Cleveleys into Fleetwood, which eventually opened as Broadway in August 1929.

The Tramroad was an important link for Cleveleys; parcels were carried on the trams until quite recently. Rossall Road in the background ran alongside the line as far as Rossall School.

Box car 16 is heading out of town in West Street, Fleetwood. The centre poles were a source of controversy from the opening of the Tramroad until they were removed in 1926.

This stretch of the line was fairly close to the sea, but Pilling Tourists wouldn't be able to see over the flood banks. The area between the Tramroad and the sea was mainly taken up by rifle ranges, and beyond them the Hutment Barracks with its massive armoury (containing 75 million rounds in 1914) which had provided most of the small-arms ammunition for the Boer War.

Fleetwood Road

Broadwater (as it's called today) was originally just "Fleetwood Road", the point where the line crossed the main highway from Poulton, which was the only road into Fleetwood before Broadway was built. This wasn't at first a major stop on the tramway, and only merited a wooden hut by the northbound track for the crossing-keeper and passengers. In 1906 it was replaced by a proper shelter on the other side of the line, which suggests that the main traffic flow was southwards rather than to Fleetwood. The Tramroad itself generated the housing development which over the years turned Fleetwood Road into Broadwater, and eventually justified a dedicated tram service between there and Fleetwood.

Fleetwood Town Centre

The Tramroad was – still is – extremely important to Fleetwood, which in the 19th Century had been entirely dependent on the railway. Fleetwood had lost most its early status as a "watering place" and become primarily a port and garrison town.

When the Tramroad opened, Fleetwood was a little world of its own, fairly remote from the rest of the coast. Hopefully not all its residents were as insular as Mrs. Mary McCall, who had

In July 1925 the tramway at Fleetwood terminus was extended to the quayside, giving passengers on the revived Pilling Tour the shortest of walks to catch the ferry. This is Box car 103 in the Blackpool Corporation fleet, formerly Tramroad car No. 22. *(AC)*

lived in Fleetwood for fifty years and told the local newspaper in 1913 that she had never seen the sea, though she had once been on the train to Thornton.

The Tramroad entered Fleetwood in the grand manner of the American interurban railways on which it was modelled – straight down Main Street. In this case it was West Street, changing to East Street halfway along – until 1911 when the Council renamed it Lord Street in a vain attempt to emulate Southport's famous boulevard. Fleetwood Council had insisted on the overhead wires being suspended from elaborately ornamented centre poles. But as road traffic increased, the poles were viewed less favourably and by 1911 the Council were asking for them to be removed. They eventually got their way, but not until 1926.

Across on the Ferry

The tracks followed the curve at Albert Square round to the terminus in North Albert Street. Passengers then had a short walk along Bold Street to catch the ferry – an ancient institution, going back to time immemorial, which on the Fylde Coast meant the 18th Century, before Fleetwood as such existed. The ferry had been run from the start by generations of the Croft family but was now operated by Fleetwood Council.

It was only a short sail across to Knott End, particularly at low tide, though Tour passengers might have to share the boat with all sorts of merchandise and livestock, since the ferry was an important lifeline to Knott End. If they

Pilling Tourists crossed from Fleetwood to Knott End on the council-operated ferry – an all-purpose vessel which served as passenger and cargo boat and sometimes Noah's Ark. For the cow in the picture, the ferry was luxury indeed; at one time cattle had to swim across the river. (AC)

timed it right, the passengers would find a horse-drawn wagonette waiting for them outside the Bourne Arms Hotel at Knott End. The wagonette was provided by Roger Ireton of the Elletson's Arms at Stakepool, near Pilling, and used on a regular service between Knott End and Pilling.

The Garstang Railway

At Pilling the wagonette took them into the yard of the Garstang & Knott End Railway, which had opened from Garstang in 1870, but hadn't yet reached its intended terminus. It was one of the more eccentric of Britain's independent light railways. The rolling stock consisted of two odd-looking engines and four unusual six-wheeled saloon coaches with balconies, which dated from the opening of the line and were reputed to be the first saloon coaches in the country.

The final leg from Pilling to the market town of Garstang needed careful timing, since there were only three return journeys a day. Even assuming the train was on time, tourists were in a quandary when they reached Garstang. If they got off there, they had only forty minutes before the train returned to Knott End. Otherwise they had to wait another four hours, though there was

In July 1904 the wagonettes which took Pilling Tourists from Knott End to Pilling were replaced by two Arrol-Johnstone motor charabancs, one of which is raising the dust in Knott End on its way back to the Ferry. They were housed in the corrugated iron shed on the right. (AC)

plenty to see in the town, especially on market day.

They could stay on the train to the main line junction at Garstang & Catterall, which gave the faint-hearted the option of travelling back to Blackpool via Preston. For those with stronger constitutions, the last return trip via Knott End didn't land its weary passengers back at Talbot Road until 8.05 p.m.

The Motor Charabancs

The Pilling Tour was no great money-spinner for the Tramroad. Receipts in its first season of 1903 were rarely more than £2 a day, equivalent to about twenty passengers at the return fare of 2s. 6d. to Garstang. There was a slightly cheaper alternative at 2s. 2d. to Pilling, missing out the Garstang & Knott End Railway, and probably much of the fun as well.

More fun was added to the Tour in 1904 when it was relaunched as the "Fylde Grand Tour" using a new motor charabanc. There were ten departures a day from Knott End, those at 10.30, 11.50 and 3.20 connecting with trains to Garstang.

The charabanc was one of the first in the country, built by the Paisley firm of Arrol-Johnstone, with steeply raked bench seats for 16 or 20 passengers (sources vary) in June 1904. It was owned by the Fleetwood Passenger Carrying Motor Company, a subsidiary of the Tramroad Company, and stored in a depot at Knott End. A second charabanc arrived soon afterwards, and a third in July 1905.

The novelty of the motor charabanc doesn't seem to have boosted the Tour much. Receipts between 14 July and 3 October 1904 were only £52. After paying £8 to Fleetwood Council for the ferry, £10 for the charabanc and £11 to the railway, the Tramroad Company were left with £23. The following year was no better, with takings of only £74 in a full season from April to October. It hardly seemed worth the effort.

In 1906, the Garstang leg was abandoned and the tour curtailed at Pilling, but when the Garstang & Knott End Railway eventually reached its goal in July 1908, the tour was re-extended to Garstang at a fare of 2s. 0d. Nevertheless receipts fell to around £50 and then slowly diminished each year until the Tour ended in 1914.

The Pilling Tour Revived

After Blackpool Corporation took over the Fleetwood Tramroad in 1920, the memory of the Pilling Tour must still have been strong, because they revived it in 1922. The fare was half a crown which, after inflation, was much better value than before, and this time the Tour was far more successful, taking £600 in 1923 and £850 in 1925. It was discontinued at the end of the 1927 season, but revived again in June 1932, still at 2s. 6d. (red and white ticket) or 2s. 0d. (green and buff) from Cleveleys. It attracted about 50 passengers a day, and took £500 in the season.

By the mid-Thirties, however, the Tour was having to compete with new attractions in Blackpool and was beginning to lose its appeal. In 1934 receipts fell to £327 and in 1935 to only £90. The fare was reduced in 1936, but to no avail, and the Pilling Tour finished at the end of that season. In its final week, the receipts amounted to 2s. 2d. - perhaps a solitary tram enthusiast making a farewell trip.

Revived Again

The final revival of the Pilling Tour came as recently as 1983, using preserved Bolton car No. 66 to Fleetwood and back, and a splendid preserved Ribble Leyland Lion which ran from Blackpool to Knott End and back, so that passengers could travel in either direction. The fare was £3.50, and the Tour operated on the first Sunday of July, August and September. It ran until 1985.

So for the fourth time in 82 years the Tour became just a part of history. And there it remains – for now. But with the Pilling Tour, you can never be sure.

Waiting for the charabanc outside the Bourne Arms at Knott End. This is one of the larger Arrol-Johnstone vehicles introduced in 1906 and registered by their builders in Paisley. The ferry landing stage is behind the camera.

The third tramway operator on the Fylde Coast was the Blackpool, St. Annes & Lytham Tramway Company, known for convenience here as the Lytham Company. Their line was a complete contrast to the other two systems in almost every respect. Although it lasted for forty years, it made no money, either for its unfortunate shareholders or for the local authority who unwisely bought the tramway in 1920 and ran it until 1937, when they replaced it by buses.

Above: Until 1905 the journey to Lytham started here at South Shore station, where one of the Lytham Company's gas cars is ready for the off. Behind the tram, in a cutting, are the station platforms and on the left one of the poles supporting the overhead wires for the Corporation's Lytham Road route. A notice in the window of the tram gives the timetable from Tuesday 1 October, which neatly dates the photograph to the winter of 1901/02. This is the seaward side of the car, showing the doors to the flywheel, the gas tanks at each end, the pipes above the windows for cooling the water, and the rudimentary controls. The inspector on the left is wearing a uniform, but the driver and conductor are distinguished only by their licence badges. *(RH)*

Below: The other terminus was in Clifton Square, Lytham, just round the corner ahead of No. 17, one of the larger cars bought when the tramway was extended from St. Annes to Lytham. No. 17 is passing the empty Market Hall on a wintry-looking day not long after the extension opened in February 1898.

"Nasty Smelly Things" - the Lytham Gas Trams

From a distance a gas car looked much like any other four-wheel tram, except that on one side it had curved panels, concealing a 4½-foot flywheel which kept the engine running at a constant speed. The car was also taller than usual, to accommodate water pipes beneath the top-deck floor for cooling the engine.

The engine itself – an orthodox two-cylinder unit producing 15 h.p. – was fed by gas from three tanks, one beneath each end of the car and the other under the side opposite the flywheel. Also under the floor was a device for de-compressing the gas from 120 lbs. per square inch, a system for injecting lubricating oil into the cylinders, and a set of friction clutches which took the drive from the engine to the wheels.

Driving

To coax this assorted ironmongery into life, the driver switched on a dynamo which provided the spark to ignite the gas in the cylinders. Next he opened the side doors and hand-cranked the fly-wheel until the engine fired. He could then return to the platform to manipulate the controls, which consisted of an orthodox tramcar handbrake and a driving lever.

When the lever was upright the friction clutches were disconnected and the engine ran under what was called "light load", with the gas igniting only on every eighth revolution of the engine, just enough to turn the flywheel - and the passengers' stomachs. Light load was used at stops and at the terminus, unless the driver chose to stop and restart the engine.

To set the car in motion, the driver moved the control lever to the right, which introduced the full supply of gas to the cylinders and connected a clutch to drive the car at nine miles per hour. To climb hills - or rather bridges since there were no hills - he pushed the lever to the left, feeding the engine with two-thirds supply of gas and connecting a separate clutch which drove the car at half speed.

Driving a gas tram was a pretty uncertain affair. If the rails were greasy and the tram full, low gear was often insufficient to surmount Skew Bridge in Lytham Road, and passengers would have to get off and walk; the energetic ones would help push the tram up.

Even on the long level stretches, driving was no sinecure. Forty years later Ted Bryning still shuddered at the memory: "I can't tell you how terrible it could be on the sandhills in winter time. For a tram to leave the track was a regular occurrence. For driver and conductor to be trying for an hour or more in a howling wind to get it back was no uncommon sight either. Driving the gas trams you had no sort of protection - unless you let the tram drive itself, and hid behind the staircase."

Riding

If driving a gas tram could be an ordeal, riding in one was infinitely worse. The gas cars probably assaulted their passengers' senses as comprehensively as any vehicle before or since.

For a start there was the noise. Even the Tramway Company admitted that "from the fact of the machinery working immediately under the floor, there is some noise under the car", though not, they insisted, "sufficient to prevent conversation in ordinary tones".

But far worse than the noise were the fumes, a sickening mixture of partly-burnt lubricating oil from the cylinders, exhaust fumes from the engine, and unburnt gas seeping from the storage tanks, especially when they were being refilled en route. After thirty years one South Shore landlady still remembered them - "nasty, smelly things, always getting out of order".

The sensations were made more nauseating by the peculiar motion of a gas tram, which paradoxically was at its worst when the car was standing still. Under "light load" the engine fired every two or three seconds, and the resultant vibration was magnified by the short wheelbase of the car so that the whole vehicle appeared to be perpetually shuddering. "What a curious arrangement the gas car is," said a Manchester newspaper in July 1897, "I don't think I like it as well as its electric cousin. There seems to be a continuous vibration which affects the whole concern, as if it were impatient to be off."

One First World War veteran, who rode the gas trams as a boy, summed it up when he swore that "a ride inside a gas tram was worse than anything I came across in France".

Women usually preferred to ride downstairs, but this group of ladies waiting for No. 17 to leave the Lytham terminus must already have experienced the lower saloon of a gas car. The crew have refilled the cooling system with water and are probably waiting for the engine to cool down. From the condition of the tram, the photograph was taken in 1898.

The Lytham Company started its operations in July 1896 with a fleet of four open-top double-deckers, powered by compressed town gas. Although stationary gas engines had been around for many years, this was the first time they had been used in Britain to drive a vehicle.

For eighteen months these four gas trams ran between South Shore and St. Annes. It was February 1898 before the line opened to Lytham, though the track had been laid from the start. A second batch of trams – larger than the originals - arrived to run the extended service.

Already the Tramway Company were in deep trouble. Most of the capital had been syphoned off by unscrupulous promoters. For years there were two holding companies and the finances became so complicated that nobody quite knew which of them owned the line. Two Annual General Meetings were held, one after the other, in the same room at the Grand Hotel, South Shore, with most shareholders attending both.

The tramway was eventually rescued by a group of Liverpool investors, but at a heavy price. All the line's future profits went to pay the interest on the Liverpool capital, leaving nothing for the ordinary shareholders.

Closure – and More Problems

The Liverpool money did at least enable the Company to abandon gas traction. The tramway closed for electrification in December 1902, but its troubles were not yet over. On 12 February 1903 one of the workmen was killed near Lytham Parish Church when he fell under a gas car towing a trailer carrying poles – the only fatality in the gas trams' history.

There was more drama two weeks later, when the worst storm for ten years demolished the tram depot on Lytham Road, fortunately at night just before the first workmen arrived. No-one was hurt but most of the gas trams were wrecked.

Re-opening with Conduit Cars

Eventually the traumatic reconstruction was finished, and the line opened again on 30 May 1903. Still the Company wasn't out of the wood. The service could only run from South Shore to Fairhaven, as the track from there into Lytham wasn't ready until a week later. For the first seven days the Lytham Company operated the service with its own ten new trams – "blue as the fairy flax" the *Lytham Times* said. These ten were all that had arrived out of an order for thirty four-wheel double-deckers.

Running the weekday service with ten trams was one thing, but the coming weekend was Whitsuntide and the Company knew that its meagre fleet

Above: **During 1896 and 1897 the gas trams ran only as far as St. Annes, where one of the original four cars is re-loading. Just to the right of the tram is St. Annes Road West. Again none of the passengers seems keen to brave the interior of the car. One of these vehicles has recently been restored after decades as a garden shed at Neath in South Wales, which bought them when Lytham electrified, and ran them until 1920. (VL)**

Below: **The "works" of a gas tram – actually one of the vehicles on the associated line at Trafford Park, but identical to the larger cars at Lytham. The two horizontal cylinders of the gas engine can be seen – directly beneath the longitudinal seats in the saloon.**

Below: **One of the last pictures of a gas tram in use. From the advanced state of the electrification work in Clifton Drive North, this picture must have been taken shortly before the line reopened in May 1903. (BL)**

Above: **Avoiding the bottom deck seems to have become quite a habit. In truth this is the first trial of an electric car on the Lytham tramway on 21 May 1903, posed with a complement of Tramway Company workmen and officials at St. Annes. The car ran from the depot to St. Thomas' Road, though one source says it went as far as Fairhaven.** *(VL)*

Below: **In 1905 the Lytham Company bought ten of these extremely rare double-deck crossbench cars to operate their extended services to Central Station, Manchester Square and Victoria Pier. The first batch, including No. 35, seen when new outside the Ship Hotel in Lytham Square, was built by the Brush Company. The following year the Company sent ten of its ordinary cars, including No. 24, to Preston to be altered to a similar style.** *(AMM)*

would be overwhelmed. So on Whit Friday, 5 June, they hired two ancient four-wheel conduit cars from the Corporation at £4 each per day. Next day the line was opened right through to Lytham, and the loan was increased to four cars, which stayed for the rest of the Bank Holiday weekend.

Even when the rest of their trams arrived, the Company had nowhere to put them until Squires Gate Depot was completed in 1904. Half the fleet had to be kept elsewhere for the winter - eight cars in the Corporation's Blundell Street shed, two at Marton and five a long way from home at Copse Road, Fleetwood.

The North Pier Steamer Tour

By the start of its second season, the Lytham Company had settled down, and

in April 1904 announced their first tourist route. For a shilling, passengers left Blackpool on one of the North Pier Steamship Company's paddle-steamers, and sailed down the coast as far as St. Annes Pier. Then they could catch any Lytham tram back through the sandhills. In those days the blue cars only ran as far as South Shore Station, so the tourists had to change to a Corporation car for the final leg to North Pier.

The tour was only available in the anti-clockwise direction - a wise precaution as the tides and the weather made steamer travel on the Fylde Coast a rather hit-and-miss affair; passengers had been known to finish up at Fleetwood, or even spend the night on board. Taking the steamer first, the passengers were reasonably certain of getting back the same day. The steamer tour only ran for one season, since the North Pier Steamship Company went into liquidation in January 1905.

The Ribble Queen Tour

The Tramway Company must have been quite taken with the idea of steamer tours, since in June 1904 they introduced another. For 1s. 9d. passengers could travel from South Shore to Preston, or for 2s. 0d. to Southport.

They went by tram to Lytham and there caught the *Ribble Queen*, a small screw steamer of 99 tons, newly built at Lytham in 1903 for the Preston firm of Monks, who ran it between Preston, Lytham and Southport. Just why anyone visiting Blackpool would want a day out at Preston is a mystery, and that leg of the tour only made sense from the Preston end, where the *Ribble Queen* was based.

The Southport run would seem to have rather more appeal. Monks claimed

The Lost Film of the Lytham Trams

Above: **The first day of electric trams in Lytham. Blackpool conduit car No. 5 unloads in the afternoon sunshine at the temporary Lytham terminus outside the Market Hall on Whit Saturday, 6 June 1903. Cars reversed here until the line was extended into Clifton Square in August. No. 5 was a particularly appropriate vehicle to introduce electric trams to Lytham, being the car which the Mayor of Manchester had driven on 29 September 1885 to inaugurate the Blackpool conduit tramway. The Mitchell & Kenyon film, from which these two pictures are taken, also shows conduit car No. 1 running down Lytham Road South, but the identity of the other two Blackpool cars used on the Lytham line that weekend is unknown. (PW)**

Below: **Trailing a cloud of dust from the newly-laid road, one of the Lytham Company's first ten electric cars bears down on two cyclists outside St. Cuthbert's Church at Lytham on 6 June 1903. The double track ended near Lowther Gardens, just behind the camera, at a point which tramwaymen always knew by the splendid name of Double Road End; from there into Lytham the electric trams used the old single track. Tramway owners were obliged by law to pave the roadway for eighteen inches on either side of the rails, which inevitably attracted the rest of the traffic onto the tram tracks. The long-suffering Lytham Company also had to provide electric street lighting, since Lytham itself had no public electricity supply until 1924. (PW)**

These pictures come from a remarkable film taken on the day the electric trams arrived in Lytham, 6 June 1903. The film was made for the Blackpool St. Annes & Lytham Tramway Company by the pioneer Blackburn firm of cinematographers, Mitchell and Kenyon, who produced documentary films of many northern towns, including one – long since lost – for the Blackpool & Fleetwood Tramroad Company.

The Lytham film began with scenes on the green and in the town centre, including unique views of Blackpool conduit cars loading and unloading in the Market Square. The main sequence was a journey on top of a tram from Lytham to South Shore.

Altogether the film was 690 feet long and lasted about twelve minutes. It was first shown at the Alhambra Theatre in Blackpool on 11 June 1903 but, like most early films, it was soon lost and forgotten. The Tramway Company's copy was unlikely to have survived, whilst the original negative presumably disappeared with Mitchell and Kenyon when they ceased production just before the First World War.

Then remarkably in June 1994, whilst Mitchell & Kenyon's old premises at Blackburn were being cleared for rebuilding, three large metal drums were saved from the rubbish skip. They turned out to contain nearly 800 rolls of 35 mm. movie film, mostly original negatives. Amongst scenes of tramways in various northern towns were several priceless sections of the 1903 Lytham film.

The surviving sequences show conduit cars in Lytham and Blackpool, as well as Lytham cars in Cambridge Road and at various points along Clifton Drive. Sadly there are no shots of Squires Gate Lane, where the cameraman was pre-occupied with filming eight newly-delivered trams being unloaded from railway wagons in the sidings at Squires Gate.

I am indebted to Peter Worden of Blackburn for providing these stills, and indeed for preserving the film, which is featured (with other historic Mitchell & Kenyon tramway footage) on "Trams in North Lancashire" published by Online Video.

that the sail from Lytham to Southport was so short that it was quicker to go by tram and then by steamer than to sail straight from Blackpool. These trips again only lasted one season; the *Ribble Queen* didn't run in 1905 and was sold in March 1906.

And that was the end of the Lytham Company's involvement with tramcar tours – as unsuccessful as the rest of the ill-starred tramway through the sandhills.

Above: The first of the Lytham Company's two short-lived tramway tours, from North Pier, only ran as far as St. Annes, but the second, to Preston and Southport via the *Ribble Queen*, involved a tram ride through to Lytham Square. Once the cars reached Ansdell, they entered a different world, as the barren soil of St. Annes gave way to the lusher vegetation of Lytham. Cars 12 and 15, in different shades of blue, pass amidst the trees in Cambridge Road, Ansdell.

Below: Lytham car 8 at the Cottage Hospital. There was a scheme to extend the track in the foreground to Preston, and another for a transporter bridge across the Ribble to Southport. As it turned out, this was as far as the trams ever ran, which left the line from Lytham Square to the Hospital too short to pay its way; in July 1926 it became the first Fylde Coast tram route to close. *(RH)*

All set to head straight through the sandhills to St. Annes, this is New South Promenade around 1934, with a Lytham open-topper turning onto the street track in Starr Gate. At the top right the Harrowside overbridge had replaced the old lane under the railway in 1930 and was met by an extension of Clifton Drive across the flattened sand dunes in 1931. Trams reversing on the crossover just north of the junction may occasionally have run down onto the southbound tram track in the foreground, but it's hard to see when the northbound track would ever be used. Another mystery is the line of sixty-odd white saloon cars on the new carriageway, though they were probably why the photograph was taken in the first place. *(SD)*

A t the start of the Thirties, Blackpool's Circular Tour seemed to be in irreversible decline, with traffic down to 100,000 passengers a year. Hopes for its revival depended on re-routing the Tour via an extended South Promenade and back along Lytham Road.

The fact that this proposal took twenty years to achieve indicates that it was no simple project. Indeed little about the extension was straightforward, either before or after it was built. One of the stranger results was that for 24 years from 1937 a complete street tramway along Starr Gate and Squires Gate Lane was kept in place solely for the Circular Tour, which until then had never owned a yard of track of its own. Stranger still that it was hardly ever used.

This street tramway sat uncomfortably in a sort of no-man's land straddling the boundary between Lytham St. Annes and Blackpool. Over the years it changed its allegiance from one side to the other and, as a result, doesn't fit naturally into the history of either town's tramways. So since the line finished up belonging to the Circular Tour, this seems a good place to tell its story, and to look at some of the other services which ran along it from time to time.

There could hardly have been a greater contrast between the two parts of this unusual line. The tramway in Starr Gate was the last new construction in Blackpool and almost the last new street line in Lancashire. But the track along Squires Gate Lane was one of the oldest tramways in the Fylde.

The Lane was a demarcation road created during the enclosure of the old common in 1767. The land to the north was allocated to landowners in Great Marton, whilst the area to the south was added to the Clifton Estate. As a result, the northern verge of the Lane became the boundary between Blackpool and Lytham St. Annes, and a source of much confusion.

Running Rights

The tram tracks in Squires Gate Lane belonged to the Blackpool St. Annes & Lytham Tramway Company. Under the 1905 through-running agreement, Blackpool Corporation were entitled to

Work on the tramway along New South Promenade began in 1925. This is the curve just south of the Pleasure Beach, with the site of the new four-track layout in the middle distance, and beyond it cars reversing at the old terminus north of the Casino building.

run their cars over the whole of the Company's track, but rarely did. Until 1917 the Corporation's Lytham Road service ran to Victoria Pier, and Blackpool cars only ran down Lytham Road South on the occasional private excursion and for special events on the land which is now Squires Gate airport.

The first of these was an extremely popular Air Pageant in October 1909, followed by a less successful one in July 1910. In August 1911 a racecourse was opened on the site, but was too short to obtain a flat-racing licence and closed in 1914.

For each of these events the Corporation ran an intensive service of special cars from North Pier through to Squires Gate at a fare of 4d. for any distance – twice the normal fare from South Shore. A photograph (too poor to reproduce) shows a row of Blackpool cars standing on the southern track in

Squires Gate Lane on 1 August 1911, waiting for crowds from the racecourse.

In 1917 the Tramway Company's lease of the line in Lytham Road South expired, and the Corporation service was extended to Squires Gate. This time, however, the cars reversed in Lytham Road itself and didn't cross the boundary into Squires Gate Lane.

New South Promenade

So despite their running powers the Corporation only became seriously involved with Squires Gate Lane in the 1920s when they completed the long-planned extension of South Promenade and its tramway along what was to become, rather unimaginatively, New South Promenade.

Until then the land south of the Star Inn consisted entirely of empty sand dunes, quite unlike the rest of Blackpool. The only road into the area was a small

lane called Harrowside which burrowed under the Coast Line railway and ran down to the beach.

The Promenade extension was 1.4 miles long and cost £330,000, though only a tenth of this was for the tram track. The new sea wall – 15 feet high and 14 feet thick at the base, was 400 feet west of the original shoreline. It was built on a foundation of tramlines lifted from North Promenade when the cantilevered reservation there was built in 1924, and driven twenty feet into the sand, eight feet apart.

When the sea wall was complete, the space behind was filled with a million cubic yards of sand. A quarter of the sand came from the beach around Victoria Pier and the rest was obtained by completely flattening the surrounding dunes, which the Corporation had bought for £90,000 after protracted negotiations. The Borough Surveyor estimated that ten per cent of the sand simply blew away.

It was ironic that in creating New South Promenade and its tramway, the Corporation destroyed the natural environment which might have made it a tourist attraction in its own right. In those days nobody bothered much about such things.

The first short portion of the new tramway opened on 1 April 1926, when an elaborate four-track layout came into operation at the Pleasure Beach, just south of the old terminus. The rest was opened by Lord Derby on 2 October 1926. At 11.40 a.m. that day, toastrack No. 82 made the first run down New South Promenade.

The Terminus that Never Was

The Corporation had intended their new tramway to continue straight across the borough boundary to St. Annes. At a meeting with Lytham St. Annes Corporation in March 1924 they

The first trams on the New South Promenade extension were Blackpool works cars like No. 3, seen here on the four-track layout at the Pleasure Beach. No. 3 was rebuilt from 1885 conduit car No. 7 in 1912. (J.M. Tomlinson)

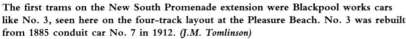

The Bottleneck - Squires Gate Lane

Above: Blue car No. 12 descends Squires Gate Lane in September 1914. The barbed-wire fence was erected by the Clifton Estate in a vain attempt to keep visitors to the 1909 Air Pageant off the sandhills. Thousands of non-paying spectators trampled across the dunes, uprooting the starr grass which bound the sand together, and creating the problem of drifting sand that plagued the Lytham trams for the rest of their days.

Below: Until New South Promenade was opened in October 1926, Squires Gate Lane was a major bottleneck on the coastal road from Preston to Blackpool. At Easter 1926, 5,000 vehicles a day were doing battle with the trams on the Lane. Here Lytham 49 and two motor cars negotiate the "double-single" track on the crest of the bridge.

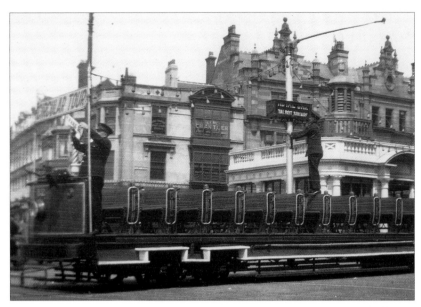

Toastrack 82 being prepared for a trip on the newly-extended Circular in 1932. The driver is fixing the fare board while the conductor changes the blind. *(R. Wilson/VL)*

proposed a combined project for a new sea-wall to join up with the existing Promenade at St. Annes. But Lytham St. Annes were unhappy about building the wall so far out, having nothing to fill the space behind it, since the sandhills between St. Annes and Squires Gate belonged to the Clifton Estate. In August 1924 Lytham St. Annes Council rejected the plan as too expensive.

This left Blackpool's new Promenade stuck out on a limb, 400 feet west of the natural coastline, and requiring an uncomfortable dog-leg to connect with Clifton Drive via a new road christened Starr Gate – "Starr" after the starr grass which abounded in the area, and "Gate" meaning road. It also made the new double-track tram terminus completely meaningless and virtually unused. Trams reversed instead at a crossover about 100 yards to the north.

In case passengers arriving from Blackpool failed to realise that this bleak spot harboured not one but two tramways, Lytham St. Annes Corporation erected an enormous banner at the bottom of Squires Gate Lane, instructing them in no uncertain terms, and in letters six feet high, to "Stand Here for Lytham St. Annes Trams".

Bridging the Gap

Unfortunately neither Lytham nor Blackpool Council were quite so unequivocal about how or when to connect their two tramways. Although the notion of extending the Circular Tour along Squires Gate Lane had been mooted before the First World War, Blackpool's legal powers covered only New South Promenade itself. It wasn't until the line was being built that they

reached agreement for a link with the Lytham tracks, via a new tramway along Starr Gate.

It seems likely that only the tracks – and not the wires – in Starr Gate and Clifton Drive were connected before July 1928. In that month Blackpool Corporation organised another Air Pageant. The Corporation were concerned that the Lytham cars would cause impossible congestion to motor traffic on Squires Gate Lane. So the wiring between Starr Gate and Clifton Drive was hurriedly completed to enable the Lytham cars to run via New South Promenade at busy times.

Rebuilding Squires Gate Lane

The connection at Starr Gate still didn't

allow Blackpool cars to run up Squires Gate Lane. The Ordnance Survey map published in 1932, but surveyed in 1930, shows the junction in Starr Gate with the right hand-fork joining Clifton Drive but the left-hand fork finishing short of the tracks in Squires Gate Lane.

Eventually in October 1930 another major project was started to widen the bridge and the rest of Squires Gate Lane. The work cost over £40,000 and wasn't completed until June 1932. The bridge was widened to the north, bringing the eastbound track onto the Blackpool side of the boundary. The tracks were maintained by Blackpool, but belonged to Lytham. Lytham also owned and maintained the overhead wires, and insisted that Blackpool use their own power via a third trolley wire, though this only lasted until May 1933.

The legalities of Squires Gate Lane were a nightmare. Walter Luff once tried to explain the situation to a confused Committee: "We pay Lytham St. Annes ½d. for every passenger carried by tramcar over Squires Gate bridge. The amount paid has been about £250 per annum. On the other hand Lytham St. Annes pay us £250 per annum for running in our area from the middle of the bridge to Lytham Road, because for book-keeping purposes we have regarded the boundary as at the end of Lytham Road whereas half the road from Lytham Road to Squires Gate is in Blackpool." And they were confused to start with.

Circular Extended

Toastrack No. 90 at last inaugurated the new Circular Tour on Saturday 14 May 1932, the start of the Whit weekend. The Tour was now 7¾ miles long, an

The extended Circular Tour was given a boost in 1934 with the arrival of twelve streamlined "Boat" cars. Here No. 225, first of the class, passes the Greyhound Stadium which opened on the Squires Gate aerodrome site in April 1933.

increase of 50%, so the Corporation raised the fare from 6d. to 9d. This turned out to be a mistake. On August Bank Holiday Sunday, usually the busiest day of the year for the Circular Tour, traffic was 40% down on 1931. By the end of the season, passenger numbers had fallen to 85,000, the lowest ever in a full season. In June 1933 the fare was reduced again to 6d. This really was value for money, and passenger figures soared back to 200,000.

New Look

Charles Furness retired as Transport Manager in 1933, and was replaced by Walter Luff, who set about revitalising the entire transport system under a Five Year Plan. In 1934 Luff gave the Circular Tour a radical new look, with the arrival of the twelve new Luxury Toastracks, or Boats as they became known. The new cars helped maintain the extended Circular's popularity, and by 1935 passenger figures had risen to 250,000.

Although there was nothing like the traffic of the Circular's Edwardian heyday - 90 trips a day was about the maximum - the Tour could still draw the crowds on a fine day. It usually ran every day from Whitsuntide onwards, unless the weather was really bad. There wasn't much demand after the Illuminations started and the Circular more or less finished at the end of September, apart from a few runs during fine October weekends.

The Squires Gate Circular

In 1935 the Corporation introduced another Circular along Squires Gate Lane. It wasn't a tourist operation, but a regular route with a ten-minute service in each direction. This Squires Gate Circular started with the summer

George Gundry, the historian of the Hastings tramways, visited Blackpool in 1934 and stayed at the Clifton Hotel overlooking Talbot Square. From the window of his room, he took this picture of new Boat car 235 positively gleaming as it loaded for the Circular Tour. *(VL)*

timetable on 8 June 1935. It ran from Talbot Square via Lytham Road to Squires Gate, then down Squires Gate Lane and back along the Promenade - and the reverse. The round trip took 38 minutes and required eight cars, usually the enclosed double-deckers 250 - 263.

By this time there were four regular services running to or through Starr Gate – Blackpool's Promenade route and the Squires Gate Circular plus two Lytham services to the Gynn, via Lytham Road or the Promenade. Each had a ten-minute frequency, which meant 42 service trams leaving or passing Starr Gate every hour. On top of this were the Circulars, which could run every five minutes on busy days.

It was hard to justify such a frenzy of activity in so barren a spot, and before long the courting couples on the sandhills had Starr Gate largely to

themselves again. The first casualty was the Squires Gate Circular. Operationally it must have been a nightmare and in traffic terms it made little sense, since nobody on the Promenade would take a tram to Lytham Road or vice versa. But it ran right through the 1935 season and restarted at Whitsuntide 1936. Then during June 1936 it died the sort of lingering death which seemed to be the fate of so many of these odd services. On some days only a single trip was made; sometimes none at all. It stopped altogether after 2 July, then ran one trip on the 7th and a final three on the 11 July.

The demise of the Squires Gate Circular didn't immediately reduce the number of Blackpool cars on Squires Gate Lane. Instead, on 3 July, the Transport Department filled the gap by extending the Promenade route from

The new turning circle at Squires Gate nears completion in August 1938. Closed and open-top Balloons on the Promenade service are reversing in Starr Gate itself, whilst in the distance a Fleetwood Rack (almost certainly No. 135) is in use as a works car.

The Battle Against the Sand

Left: Ever since the sandhills were damaged by spectators during the 1909 Air Pageant, and again by troops in the First World War, the Lytham tramways had to fight a constant battle to keep the tracks around Starr Gate clear of blowing sand.

On a blustery 6 July 1935, a Lytham car swings into Starr Gate past the Lytham St. Annes banner, on its way from Squires Gate depot to take up service on the St. Annes – Gynn route. In the distance works car 26 is running up and down Clifton Drive to keep the track clear of sand. (*Dr. Hugh Nicol, National Tramway Museum*)

Centre: A few minutes later No. 26 arrives at Starr Gate, and its driver turns the trolley for another run. No. 26 had been fitted with temporary brushes to clear the sand in December 1923, and then in November 1925 lost its top-deck to become a full-time works car. (*Dr. Hugh Nicol, National Tramway Museum*)

Below: No. 26 may have won its brief skirmish with the sand on 6 July, but three months later, on 18 October 1935, Mother Nature struck back with the worst sand-storm ever to hit the Starr Gate area. Winds up to 70 miles per hour blew more than 4,000 tons of sand onto the tram lines in Clifton Drive, and even closed the coastal railway for a time.

It took three days to clear the tram tracks. When the council realised that the task was beyond them, they invited local builders – who normally paid for their sand - to take away as much as they could carry. A fleet of wagons rapidly descended on the Drive.

It was, as they say, an ill wind …

Starr Gate up the Lane to reverse on the crossover outside the depot. They set a fare of a penny from Starr Gate to the depot, though it's unlikely that they sold many tickets. This extension was as short-lived as the Squires Gate Circular, lasting only for the 1936 season.

Last Fling

In April 1937 the Lytham St. Annes trams were replaced by buses, and the tracks in Clifton Drive and along two sides of the triangular junction at Starr Gate were abandoned. Although this reduced pressure on the street track in Starr Gate, it still made a very unsatisfactory terminus, and in September 1938 was replaced by a sleeper-track turning circle. The westbound track in Starr Gate and Squires Gate Lane now wasn't used at all, and the eastbound track only by the Circular Tour in summer.

Traffic on the Tour was falling again despite having new cars and a new route. Passengers were down to 125,000 in 1938, which was a poor year for Blackpool in general. Perversely the 1939 season, when war had become inevitable, was much better and on August Bank Holiday Monday more than a hundred tours were operated - the highest for many years.

As in 1914, the Corporation didn't intend to give up the Illuminations just because of a war, insisting that they could switch the Lights off in a few seconds if there was an air-raid warning. But wiser counsels prevailed and when war was declared on 3 September, the season came to a premature end. A few Circular Tours ran each day until 12 September, then four more on the 25th and a final solitary trip on the 27th. It looked like the end of the Circular Tour "for the duration".

But not quite. At the start of the 1940 season, visitors still flocked to Blackpool. This was the period of the Phoney War, and road traffic into the resort at Easter was only 20% down on 1938. The Circular almost certainly ran at some time during the weekend, and it's known that ten toastracks were out on the Sunday. It's hard to be sure because Easter Sunday fell on 24 March, and the financial year ended on 31 March, so the traffic receipts for the holiday weekend are lost within the 1939/40 figures.

Intriguingly the receipts for 1940/41 show £35 from the Circular Tour. Perhaps some innocent depot inspector sent out the Circulars at Whitsuntide 1940, just as he had always done. If so, it would be nice to think that these clandestine Circular Tours brightened up a nervous Bank Holiday for somebody, because there weren't going to be any

Even after the Second World War, Starr Gate was largely undeveloped. The Squires Gate Hotel at the corner of Squires Gate Lane and Clifton Drive – first announced in 1897 – finally materialised in 1938, the same year as the private hotel opposite the tram turning circle. During the war the northbound curve on the circle was re-aligned to make room for a siding to serve a rifle range just west of the tram tracks. The siding was removed in 1949/50. In the foreground the old stub terminal had been lifted when the circle was built in 1938. *(AMM)*

more for a very long time.

In Limbo

With the end of the Circular Tour, the tracks in Starr Gate and Squires Gate Lane fell out of use completely. They weren't officially abandoned, however, as they provided access to the Lytham Depot should the war make it necessary to store Blackpool cars there. As far as is known, no tram ran up or down Squires Gate Lane for another ten years, though it's possible that an occasional run was made to maintain the right of way.

The next documented use of Squires Gate Lane came on the morning of 9 January 1950. After complaints from the trade union about the lack of toilets at Squires Gate terminus, the double-deckers on the Lytham Road service

were extended down the Lane to the depot, which now housed the Lytham St. Annes bus fleet.

Before the morning was out, Walter Luff received a telephone call from Woodhead's Garage opposite the depot, complaining that the standing trams were damaging their trade. On this somewhat flimsy basis, Luff immediately cut the trams back to Lytham Road.

Luff told the next Transport Committee meeting that he intended to extend the Lytham Road cars further down Squires Gate Lane "to a point near Starr Gate", presumably to reverse on the single track in the street, but nothing came of it.

Revival

Walter Luff retired in 1954 and was

Boat car 226 leaves the short single-track section of Starr Gate in 1960, the last year of the Circular Tour. Thirty years after the line was built, there were still very few buildings at Starr Gate. *(F.W. Ivey)*

The Promenade Circular might have been a pale imitation of the genuine Circular Tour, but it still attracted a sizeable queue at the Tower on a warm June evening in 1961. *(Brian Turner)*

succeeded by Joe Franklin. Just like his two predecessors when they took office, Franklin set about reviving the Circular. In Franklin's case this enthusiasm was all the more remarkable since the Tour hadn't run for fourteen years.

In May 1957 the Corporation announced the revival of the Circular Tour and the re-opening of the eastbound track in Squires Gate Lane. Test runs were made with two types of double-decker (which must have been a Balloon and a Standard) and two single-deckers (presumably a Boat and a railcoach).

On 9 July the Tour re-started, using six open Boat cars which loaded in Talbot Square and picked up at Central Station and Pleasure Beach. The fare was 1s. 3d. It was astonishing to see Circular Tour trams lining up in Talbot Square, just as they had done all those years ago. On August Bank Holiday all twelve Boats were running on the Tour.

By the end of the 1957 season, 1,019 trips had been run and 50,000 passengers carried. The revenue of £2,843 was a drop in the ocean amongst the total tramway income of £500,000, but it was a vindication of Joe Franklin's enterprise in reviving the tour. If only Walter Luff had done it earlier.

In 1958 the Circular started at Whit and operated right through the season -

just like the old days - running nearly 2,000 tours. Passenger figures rose to 75,000, and in 1959 to 108,000 with almost 3,000 journeys. It looked as if the Tour was building back up to its pre-war popularity. The Corporation had even bought large advertising posters in the traditional style.

The Promenade Circular

But suddenly there was competition. A new "Circular Tour" started briefly at Easter 1960 and then ran regularly from 29 May. It loaded on the middle track at the Tower, ran up to Little Bispham turning circle, where the guards sometimes announced that "this is the Circular bit". From there the Tour went down to the circle at Starr Gate and then returned to the Tower.

This was the third straight-up-and-down tour which Joe Franklin had introduced, starting in 1956 with the Tour of Illuminations *(opposite)* which followed the same route as the Promenade Circular, and then the Coastal Tour *(page 58)* to Fleetwood, using the prototype twin-car in 1958.

The Promenade Circular, as it became known, used all sorts of rolling stock - rather like the original Circular in its heyday. In fine weather the Boats were favourites, of course, but many other classes appeared, including three of the

cars restored for the 75th Anniversary of the tramways in 1960.

The End

This cuckoo in the Circular nest rapidly outgrew the original tour, which restarted on 5 June 1960, but was only a shadow of its former self for the rest of the season, running mainly on Sundays.

Behind the scenes the Transport Department were planning to abandon the Lytham Road line in October 1961 and the other street routes soon afterwards. The closure plan wasn't officially announced until October 1960, but it looks suspiciously as though the Circular Tour was switched to the Promenade to ease the closing of the inland routes.

Whatever the machinations, the Circular Tour was prematurely abandoned, almost by default. The Tour simply never restarted at the beginning of the 1961 season, though all the track remained usable until the Squires Gate route closed on 29 October. It turned out that the last journeys had been made on Sunday 11 September 1960, when three Boats ran a total of seven trips.

After 55 years the greatest Circular Tour of them all had passed into history. And nobody said goodbye.

The Illuminations Tour

Blackpool had run Illuminations Tours since 1930, but always by bus - an unsatisfactory arrangement, particularly at the weekend, when the Promenade became one-way and the buses had to return via Devonshire Road and Whitegate Drive. However there were plenty of spare buses in the evening, whereas the tram fleet was already stretched to its limits during the Lights, and had to be augmented by hiring cars from Lytham St. Annes.

When the Illuminations Tour by tram did finally start on 6 September 1956, it was only made possible by bringing the last surviving Standard double-deckers out of retirement. On the first Saturday of the Lights, there were six Standards on the tour - Nos. 41, 42, 48, 143, 147 and 158. Four others - 28, 49, 159 and 177 - appeared soon after, and subsequently cars 40 and 160, which had been withdrawn, were re-licensed and returned to the fleet.

The Illuminations Tour gave the Standards a new lease of life and, as it turned out, extended their careers long enough for several of them to be

The Tour of Illuminations was operated initially by the traditional Blackpool Standard cars. They served from 1956 until 1966; this is No. 147 arriving at Bispham in September 1966 on the very last run by a Standard, apart from the two illuminated cars 158 and 159, which survived for a few more weeks. *(Brian Turner)*

preserved. The last three - 147, 158 and 159 - survived until the 1966 Illuminations.

Initially the Tour ran only as far as Bispham, where the Lights ended, but to reduce congestion there, and save passengers turning their seats, it was soon extended to Little Bispham, probably the first time fare-paying passengers had travelled round the turning circle there.

Double-deckers were always preferred on the Tour of Illuminations, but over the years almost every car in the fleet must have appeared on it at some time: restored cars were particularly popular. From 1959 the illuminated cars themselves ran on the Tour at a premium fare. That first year, they carried 11,000 passengers and took £1,800.

Compared to the traditional Circular round Marton, the Illuminations Tour was expensive - the fare in 1956 was 2s. 0d. on weekdays and 2s. 6d. on Saturday and Sunday, and went up by 6d. in 1957. In 1959 the Tour trams carried 125,000 passengers in six weeks, and earned £18,000. The revenue was astronomical, even by Blackpool's standards, averaging 14s. 7d. per mile, four times normal.

The Tour operated successfully for more than forty years, but during the 1990s its popularity waned as more and more visitors bought Travelcards which allowed them unlimited mileage on the normal trams. Nowadays most of the journeys are made by the illuminated cars themselves.

The modern equivalent of the Standard cars on the Illuminations Tour were the two Jubilee cars, 761 and 762, rebuilt from double-deck Balloon cars. No. 761 waits at North Pier to load for one of its first Tours after entering service in 1979. *(Brian Turner)*

The Coastal Tour

The Coastal Tour was introduced in 1958 specifically for the prototype twin-car which had been converted at Rigby Road from railcoaches 275 and 276.

Until the rest of the twin-car fleet emerged in 1960 and 1961, the prototype was rather an awkward proposition. It was twice as long as the rest of the fleet, twice as long as most of the stops on the Fleetwood Tramroad, and could only reverse at four places on the system. To make matters worse the trade union had "blacked" it from working in normal service while they negotiated extra pay for the driver.

So the Coastal Tour, which started on 24 May 1958, was to some extent a virtue made out of necessity. The Tour covered 22 miles - the whole length of the tramway between Starr Gate and Fleetwood. There were turning circles at both ends, and passengers were only allowed to board at Talbot Square, Central Station, Pleasure Beach, Starr Gate and Bispham, so the twin-car didn't need to stop at any awkward places.

In its first two seasons, the Coastal Tour was surprisingly popular. The solitary twin-car ran about 300 trips each year and carried 16,000 passengers, giving receipts of 6s. 8d. per mile, compared to 5s. 0d. a mile when the set ran on other duties.

The styling of the twin-car was a surprisingly successful compromise between the main body of the English Electric railcoach, which was the basis of the conversion, and the front end of the Coronation cars, one of which is seen in the background at the Tower in 1958.

The Tour continued to operate when the other twin-cars appeared, from July 1960 onwards, and was still being advertised in 1966 at a fare of 4s. 0d. and the proviso that "Tours will be operated in reverse direction when required", which had appeared since the Tour started. This option doesn't ever seem to have been invoked, though it wouldn't have been easy to tell which way a Tour car was going unless it stopped for passengers.

Like the Promenade Circular, the Coastal Tour quietly disappeared. It was one of those operations which inspectors could run as and when appropriate, and nobody seems to know just when it last operated - probably in the late Sixties.

The prototype trailer car, No. 275 – its wheels painted white in best railway tradition - waits with No. 276 at North Pier for an official party to sample the Coastal Tour in 1958. No. 275 was rebuilt as a towing car in 1961.

7. Brighton's Exclusive Tourist Car

From time to time Brighton operated illuminated cars round its Tourist route. This is car 1 in the depot yard at Lewes Road, with a dapper two-man crew. Brighton normally had several cars illuminated in a similar style with about 250 bulbs, but the flags and top-deck lights on No. 1 are an extra, presumably for the Coronation in June 1911.

On 1 June 1905, just nine days before Blackpool Corporation introduced their Circular Tour, William Marsh, acting Manager of the Brighton Corporation Tramways, presented his Tramways Committee with a proposal for a Tourist Car.

Brighton's narrow-gauge tramway was about the same size as Blackpool's, but very different in shape. The frontage of the town was relatively small, and much of the promenade was actually in the adjoining borough of Hove. As a result residential development went inland rather than along the seafront - and the tramways likewise.

Fortunately Brighton's streets were fairly wide and straight, and most of the routes were double-track – one of the advantages of the 3 ft. 6 ins. gauge. They were also extremely steep, rising as high as 400 feet, with one section of 1-in-9 and long stretches at 1-in-12½; after Halifax, Brighton was said to have the hilliest tramway system in the country. Like most South Coast systems, Brighton

only ever ran four-wheeled open-toppers, but built its own cars, and was generally a more progressive outfit than most in the region.

Tourist Cars Proposed

As evidence of this, Brighton could claim to have introduced the first dedicated tourist route in Britain. Although the Blackpool Circular started a month earlier, it didn't become a genuine tourist operation until the trams stopped running to a timetable in 1907.

The proposal which Marsh put to the Brighton Committee was just the opposite of Blackpool's Circular. Instead of a regular all-day service, Marsh proposed just a single departure every morning from Monday to Saturday. The tour would cost a shilling – three times the Blackpool fare – and would cover all

routes except Lewes Road, which was flat, Queen's Park, which had single track, and the Station route, which was too short.

"The Tourist Car would fill a decided want as expressed by many visitors," Marsh reported, "Provided an average of ten passengers could be obtained every day, it would pay all expenses, including advertising." On 5 June the Committee approved the plan with such enthusiasm that they asked for an afternoon departure as well. A week later Marsh was appointed Tramways Manager, a post he was to hold for 34 years.

Special Conductors

In his proposal Marsh had suggested that "it would tend to encourage passengers if a Conductor who is well versed in the chief places of interest on the route

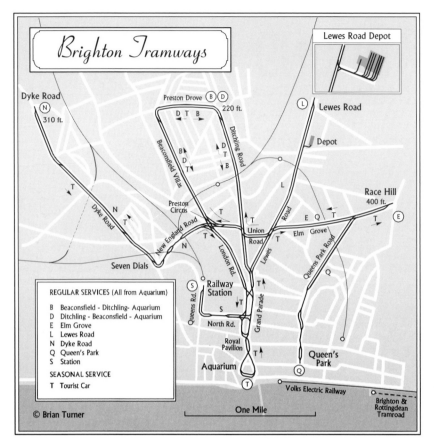

REGULAR SERVICES (All from Aquarium)

B   Beaconsfield - Ditchling- Aquarium
D   Ditchling - Beaconsfield - Aquarium
E   Elm Grove
L   Lewes Road
N   Dyke Road
Q   Queen's Park
S   Station

SEASONAL SERVICE

T   Tourist Car

© Brian Turner

Lewes Road as far as Elm Grove, where it turned right, up a continuous 1-in-12½ gradient to the Race Hill terminus, 400 feet above sea level. There the tram waited about 15 minutes whilst the conductor took the passengers to the racecourse grand-stand and "showed them the surrounding countryside", which was really an excuse to get them out of the way while the trolley was turned and the seats reversed.

Returning down Elm Grove, the Tourist Car ran along Union Road - only otherwise used for depot workings - before turning right up Ditchling Road, along Preston Drove and back via Beaconsfield Villas to Preston Circus. There it reversed once more – this time with passengers on board. It then started climbing again to Dyke Road terminus, where there was another 15-minute break "to admire the view" before returning to the Aquarium. The nine-mile trip took about 1¾ hours, since the cars rarely travelled at more than half-speed.

The First Season

In its first six-day week - it never ran on Sundays - the Tourist service carried 445 adults and 26 children, which worked out at 39 passengers per departure, and regularly required the use of a duplicate tram. The revenue per mile was three times the average for the system.

During the third week of the service, to coincide with a programme of motor racing in the town, the Corporation operated four illuminated cars (with about 250 lamps on each) every evening round the tourist route, though it isn't clear whether they carried passengers. It was the start of a long Brighton tradition of illuminated trams.

As the 1905 season reached its August peak, demand increased to the point where four cars were needed for each departure. Two of them probably went the opposite way round the circuit, an option which the Corporation always mentioned in their publicity.

For most of the August Race Week - traditionally the busiest time of the year for the Brighton trams - the Tourist service had to be discontinued because of its disruptive effect on the hectic traffic to Race Hill - or vice versa. But on the one day it did run, Friday 11 August, it carried an all-time daily record of 234 passengers.

Although in later years the Tourist service was worked by cars from the Beaconsfield Road/Ditchling Road circular, during its first season it was operated by route"S"cars,which normally ran to the railway station. On 12 September 1905 a group of passengers boarded a Tourist Car at the Aquarium

travelled on the top, describing everything as the car passed". In the four weeks before the tour started, Marsh chose two of these "Special Conductors" and sent them off to Brighton Library to brush up on their local history.

The Route

At 11 a.m. on 3 July 1905 the first

Tourist Car set off from the Aquarium. Or rather Tourist Cars, because there were more passengers waiting than could be accommodated on the 26 outside seats of a Brighton four-wheeler, and a duplicate car had to be organised.

Leaving the Aquarium, the Tourist Car negotiated the one-way layout past the Royal Pavilion before heading along

The Special Conductor waits on the top deck as Brighton's Tourist Car prepares to set out on its nine-mile journey from the Aquarium, where all the Brighton trams started. Because the terminus was a continuous loop, passengers approaching from the promenade couldn't see the front destinations of the trams, so Brighton had a unique arrangement of route letters mounted on a board in the centre of the top deck. The Tourist Car was route "T", though No. 27 isn't carrying a board.

25 minutes before its departure time, and were surprised to find that it was scheduled to make another trip on route "S" first. In view of the crowd waiting at the Aquarium, they opted to ride to the station and back for a penny each way rather than lose their seats on the Tour.

Passing the Hat Round

At the end of its first year, the Tourist service had carried 12,222 passengers and was adjudged a great success. The Special Conductor received something of a mixed reaction. His rôle, according to the Corporation's publicity, was to "accompany each Car, and describe in a loud voice all the places of interest passed, give a short history of the town, and do his best to interest and amuse the passengers". The *Brighton Herald* commended the Conductor's diplomacy when passing what he described as "The Home for the Aged Poor, otherwise known as the Workhouse".

But the Corporation were concerned that the Conductors had been passing the hat round in the traditional manner at the end of the Tour. One councillor said that since the men had worked their way up to be Conductors of Tourist Cars, and had to point out 160 places of interest, they were entitled to some little extra remuneration. In the end, notices were placed on the cars "prohibiting the giving of gratuities", which satisfied municipal sensitivities but probably made little difference.

According to one correspondent to the *Herald,* the Special Conductors received 5d. extra per day, which he thought scant reward for increasing the revenue three-fold. One of the Conductors said in 1905 that the Tours were a great advertisement for Brighton, and that so far he had carried visitors from Florida, South Africa, Japan, Russia and Australia, not to mention tramway officials from Leeds, Bradford, Halifax, East Ham, Southampton, Hastings, Croydon, Portsmouth, Erith, Glasgow, Stockton, South Shields and Leicester. If these tramways were thinking of copying the idea, none of them did.

Wartime Setback

Although it never quite achieved the same popularity as during its first season, the Tourist Car continued in similar vein for more than twenty years, carrying around 8,000 passengers a year with revenue of about £500.

As in Blackpool, the Tourist service was badly hit initially when the First World War broke out, but soon recovered and in 1916 carried 8,633 passengers and took £412. Brighton, again like Blackpool, suffered from deferred maintenance and high passenger

The first stop on Brighton's Tourist route was at Race Hill, where passengers disembarked for a tour of the grandstand, whilst the crew reversed the seats and the trolley for the journey back to town. During Race Week each August, the Brighton trams carried huge numbers of passengers up the steep hill to the racecourse.

demand from the billeting of troops. Passenger traffic doubled during the war, and there were insufficient serviceable trams to operate the normal service, let alone the Tourist Car, which was withdrawn after the Easter 1917 holiday. The Tour didn't run at all in 1918 but was back on the rails in 1919, carrying 9,299 passengers. Next season the fare was increased from 1s. 0d. to 1s. 6d. and passenger figures almost halved.

Decline

Thereafter the Tour was on a downward slope until 1925, when only 2,652 passengers were carried. Motor coaches were offering more adventurous trips than a ride round the Brighton suburbs, and it was decided that the Tour had had its day. The last Tourist Car ran in

October 1925. It was remarkable that the service had adhered so faithfully to the original concept which William Marsh had first outlined twenty years before.

The Brighton system itself continued serenely on under Marsh's management, still building open-top four-wheelers as late as 1937. The end, when it arrived, came suddenly. In April 1939 the Corporation agreed a co-ordinated transport scheme with the Brighton Hove & District Omnibus Company, which was implemented with brutal swiftness. Within four months the entire system was replaced by trolleybuses, and seventy trams - many of them almost new - were scrapped. William Marsh retired, saddened at the tragic disappearance of his life's work - the last seaside tramway on the South Coast.

A special tour of the Brighton tramways was laid on for a group of French visitors as part of the Entente Cordial in 1907. A procession of decorated cars leaves the railway station, led by cars 32 and 35. (BR)

Above: The ultimate in seaside tram rides. Between 1896 and 1901 the Brighton & Rottingdean Seashore Electric Tramroad operated this remarkable sea-going tram, officially named "Pioneer" but popularly known as "Daddy Long-legs". It ran for three miles through water up to sixteen feet deep between a landing stage at Brighton and a pier at Rottingdean, for a fare of 6d. each way. The rails were eighteen feet apart, and the car travelled at about five miles per hour. The Board of Trade insisted that the tram carry a lifeboat – just visible, suspended from davits at the far end of the car. *(Brighton Library)*

Below: Volks Electric Railway (named after its originator Magnus Volk, who also built the Rottingdean line) was the earliest and longest-lived of all seaside electric tramways, opened in 1883 and still running. Since this picture was taken, c. 1920, the shingle has built up to the level of the tracks. Massed in the background are the charabancs which killed off Brighton's Tourist Car.

The summer of 1905 saw the launch of three tourist operations within the space of two months, starting with Blackpool's Circular route on 10 June, and Brighton's Tourist Car on 3 July. On 31 July the Hastings Tramway Company eclipsed them both with a tourist route which was twice as long as Blackpool's, 100 feet higher than Brighton's and a good deal more scenic than either of them.

Whether it was a Circular Tour or just a circular route is debatable. The

Car 14, travelling anti-clockwise round the Hastings Circular, passes the post office in the village of Baldslow at the north-western extremity of the route. Several of the passing loops along the country roads were out of sight of each other, and trams only met at pre-ordained places according to the timetable, which didn't make it easy to operate extra cars to meet exceptional demands. (DP)

Tramway Company themselves couldn't make up their minds. The round-trip tickets called it a Circular Tour, but the trams - orthodox open-top four-wheelers - showed "Circular Route" on the blind and on boards along the top-deck sides. In later years the boards seem to have disappeared, and the front blinds showed different destinations outwards and

inwards.

The Hastings Company's 3 ft. 6 ins. gauge system was the largest seaside tramway in Britain for much of the Edwardian period, with slightly more cars than Blackpool Corporation, and a lot more miles. The Circular, unusually, was the first route to open. Many of the drivers were poached from Brighton, a common practice in those days - Brighton had done the same when its tramways started.

The Hastings Circular was nine miles long and ran for much of the way along rural by-ways, reaching a height of 500

Car 9 on the opening day, 31 July 1905, at Ore. In the early days the cars displayed "Circular Route" on their blinds, but later they showed separate destinations outwards and inwards.

The tickets for the Hastings route referred to it as a "Circular Tour". This one was issued on 21 October 1923. It was black on white, with "Circular Tour" over-printed in red, apparently by a rubber stamp. The fare had risen from 6d. to 1s. 0d. after the war. (DP)

Car 9 again, with a posse of cyclists following the car through the depths of the
Sussex countryside near Ivy House Lane during a trial run in July 1905, before the
Circular route opened. *(DP)*

feet through the Sussex countryside. The
round trip fare was a very reasonable 6d.,
which rose to 1s. 0d. after the war.
Unfortunately the single-track layout
proved extremely restrictive. Each circuit
of the route involved negotiating more
than seventy sets of points, which meant
that the Hastings Circular was never
really able to fulfil the potential which its
scenic nature promised.

The Dolter System

The Circular also laboured under the
disadvantage of not running along the
Front. There were tram tracks right along
the main promenade (and westwards to
Bexhill and Cooden) but the Circular
couldn't use them, because Hastings
Council refused to allow the Tramway
Company to erect overhead wires on this
prestigious stretch of the coast. The
Company, shuddering at the expense of a
conduit and knowing the problems that
Blackpool had experienced on its seafront
line, seized on a relatively new
technology which had been introduced at
Paris in 1902.

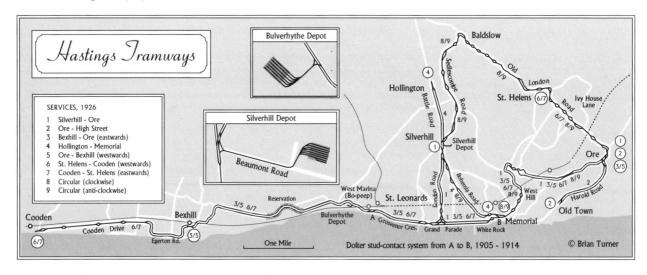

The smock mill (since demolished) at Baldslow, 436 feet above sea level. The Circular
car, heading west on an anti-clockwise circuit, is just about to drop down into the
village shown on page 63. *(DP)*

The use of this Dolter stud-contact
system *(see opposite)* effectively divided the
system into two – the coastal line to
Bexhill, which used a batch of some
twenty cars equipped for both the Dolter
and overhead systems, and the inland
routes which used conventional cars.
Each section had its own depot.

Out of the Frying-pan

By 1913 the Board of Trade had lost
patience with the Dolter system and told
the Hastings Company to find a
replacement. Instead of converting to
overhead wires, the Company chose
another untried means of propulsion –
petrol-electric traction, which replaced
the Dolter equipment in March 1914.

This was not the same system as the
Leyland petrol cars running between
Morecambe and Heysham *(page 96)* on

The Dolter Stud-Contact System

GRAND PARADE. ST. LEONARDS

Above: Hastings chose the Dolter stud-contact system for its route along the seafront at St. Leonards, although the rest of the system used conventional overhead wires. This is the junction with the London Road line, whose wires can be seen briefly intruding on the hallowed ground. Car 42 is setting off westward along the Dolter line; hanging from its fender is the safety-brush to detect leaking studs. In the distance the track briefly became single to run behind the Colonnade, before returning to the sea-front.

Below: The view eastwards from the Colonnade along the same length of track. These two cars are running a local service from the Memorial to the western end of the Dolter tracks. The side boards on the trams called the destination Bopeep (after the Bopeep Inn) whilst the end blinds called it West Marina (after the railway station of that name). The body of car 43 has been recovered for eventual restoration. As yet nobody has suggested restoring a portion of the Dolter system for it to run on - but stranger things have happened in the world of tramcar preservation.

The Dolter system, named after its French inventor, consisted of a row of studs, nine feet apart, between the rails. As the tram passed over a stud, a 12-foot long magnetic skate under the car attracted a lever inside the stud, connecting it to the 550V supply. Once the tram passed, the lever fell back and switched the stud off. At least that was the theory.

In practice the tide or spray corroded the studs, so that they no longer switched on and off properly. If two adjacent studs remained dead, the tram lost its power, and often stopped altogether. But the worst problem was with studs which didn't switch off properly. There were fuses to prevent a stud remaining completely live at 550V, but sometimes the switches in the stud stayed partly open, leaking sufficient current to give a pedestrian – or more usually a horse – an unpleasant shock.

To detect leaking studs, the trams had a safety-brush hanging from the back fender, which rang a bell if it detected any current. The driver would stop the car whilst the conductor attacked the errant stud with a mallet until the lever fell back properly. Then the driver had to reverse and run over the stud again to check that it was dead. If it wasn't, he covered the stud with a leather mask until it could be repaired; in the meantime the driver of every tram had to remove and replace the mask.

The only British tramways to use the Dolter were Hastings (1905 - 1914), Torquay (1907 - 1911) and Mexborough & Swinton in Yorkshire (1907 - 1908).

HASTINGS & BOPEEP

Above: **Looking at this stylish Edwardian scene by the bandstand, it's easy to see why Hastings Town Council were reluctant to allow overhead wires along their sea-front. Unfortunately the Dolter stud–contact system, which promised so much, created more problems than it solved. Besides being temperamental, it was liable to impart a substantial electric shock to anyone - man or beast - who stepped on a faulty stud. So instead of travelling along the well-paved tram tracks, as happened in most other towns, horse-drawn traffic in Hastings gave them a very wide berth.** *(Judges)*

Below: **When Hastings abandoned the Dolter system in 1914, they fitted the Bexhill trams with the Tilling-Stevens petrol-electric system, which was more commonly used on buses. This wartime view of car 42 shows the exhaust pipe running above the saloon windows.** *(DP)*

which the petrol engine drove the wheels directly. At Hastings the engine drove a generator connected to the normal electric motors. The equipment, already used on motor buses, was known as the Tilling-Stevens system and became popular on buses in the Twenties, Blackpool being a regular customer. As with the Dolter system, the Hastings trams only used their petrol engines over a short section of the route.

The main disadvantage, when applied to a double-ended tram, was the exhaust. Going in one direction the exhaust disappeared satisfactorily behind the tram, but going the other way the fumes were blown back into the saloon. Nevertheless the petrol-electric cars soldiered on through the war until Hastings Council finally allowed overhead wires to be strung along the Front. It was March 1921 before the installation was complete and Hastings' two tramway systems could finally operate as one.

Trolleybus Circular

Whilst all this was going on, the Hastings Circular had been operating happily enough on the orthodox part of the tramway system, but once the petrol cars had gone and the wires were strung along the seafront, some of the Circular journeys were diverted via London Road and the sea-front, at a fare of 1s. 2d. instead of 1s. 0d.

Unfortunately the Hastings tramways had a very short life - only 24 years altogether. The Circular route closed on 30 September 1928, and the final fragment of the system finished without ceremony on 13 March 1929 - the first seaside electric tramway in Britain to be abandoned.

This wasn't the end of the Circular route, however, for on 15 May 1929 it re-opened as a trolleybus service. At first it even had that rarest of vehicles, the open-top trolleybus. It was ironic that a resort with such sensibilities about overhead wiring should now have double trolleybus wires along its Front.

The trolleybus Circular ran for another 30 years before closing, with the rest of the system, on 31 May 1959, by which time the Hastings route had covered almost exactly the same span as Blackpool's Circular Tour. However its 54 years with electric traction was, by a long way, a record for a circular route.

9. Torquay : Tours Without Wires

The next resort to introduce a tourist operation was another narrow-gauge South Coast tramway. The Torquay Tramways Company's system had much in common with Hastings, including a level coastal line and a hilly Circular.

Torquay Council hadn't been sure that they wanted trams at all, let alone with overhead wires, so they had been following Hastings' involvement with the Dolter system very closely. Unfortunately by the time the deficiencies of the Dolter became apparent, Torquay had committed themselves to it, not just for the seafront, but for the entire system.

Construction didn't begin until 1905 and ominously took eighteen months, so that it was April 1907 before the first route opened, making Torquay almost the last new seaside tramway in Britain. On 11 November 1907 a Circular route through Babbacombe was completed. Normally trams showed the destination "Circular Route", but the ceremonial first car showed "Circular Tour" which suggests that the Tramways Company were already intending to promote the route as a tourist attraction, much as Hastings had done.

Tourist Cars

In fact the Company were planning, not just a Hastings-style Circular, but an up-market Tourist Car similar to Brighton's.

Above: **Low winter sunshine gives an unusually clear view of this brand-new Torquay car's mechanical equipment. Behind the central slipper-brake is the magnetic skate (twelve feet long and weighing a ton) which activated the Dolter studs and picked up the current. This picture of a car on test at the Strand was posted on 19 January 1907, eleven weeks before the Torquay tramways eventually opened. Unfortunately the message on the card, from Emma to Winnie, sheds little light on what was going on: "I thought you would like this for your collection. Don't you think that young man next to the P.C. is like my cousin Ern?"**

Below: **The Torquay tramways opened at last on 4 April 1907 - the last new tramway in the South of England. Three cars - Nos. 13, 4 and 18 - are setting off from Beacon Quay on the inaugural journey. Hanging from No. 13's fender is the Dolter safety-brush, as used on the Hastings cars and described in Chapter Eight.**

Overleaf: **Every August, Torquay's Regatta Fair took over the streets by the harbour, blocking the tracks to Beacon Quay. Car 23 is on the Circular route in 1922. A notice on the pole advertises the Tourist cars at a shilling.** *(Hulton Getty)*

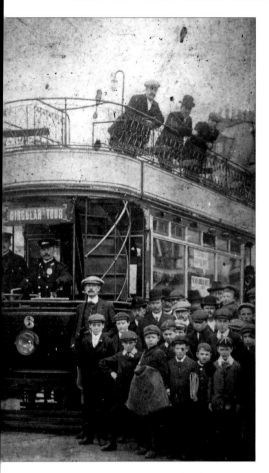

Above: **This is believed to be the inaugural car on Torquay's Circular round Babbacombe on 11 November 1907. A notice in the window refers to the "New Circular Route" but the destination indicator suggests that Torquay always intended to run a tourist service round the circle.**

Below: **A Tourist Car on Torquay's Dolter stud-contact system. Unlike Hastings, the entire Torquay system was run on the Dolter, so the trams had no trolleys. The picture is thought to have been taken at Torre Station.**

It isn't known for sure just when Torquay's Tourist Car started running, but it was probably in 1908, the first season after the Circular route opened. Its *modus operandi* was laid down in the Company's Rules and Regulations issued in April 1911:

TOURIST CAR – This car must be treated as a "special" car, and as such must, if necessary, give way to all "service" cars. Service cars, however, must assist as far as possible in ensuring an unbroken run for the Tourist Car. This Car is run with the object of giving visitors an opportunity of viewing Torquay as far as possible from the tram routes, and also of giving aged people and invalids a comfortable ride extending over the period of time advertised. It is essential therefore:
(1) That the Car be driven at an even rate of speed, not to exceed eight miles per hour at any part of the route.
(2) That there should be no lurching through points or around curves.
(3) That particular care should be exercised by the Motorman and Conductor and others in keeping this car and its equipment clean, and its working parts in good and smooth working order.

The tram itself would be one of Torquay's standard four-wheel open-toppers, though the Rule Book rather implies that one particular vehicle was dedicated to the operation. The Tourist Cars started right at the centre of the tramway system, by the Clock Tower, probably loading on the south-to-east curve, which wasn't normally used and was eventually removed.

Although the precise itinerary isn't known, the Tour seems to have covered the line to Torre Station, a trip round the Babbacombe circle and a run along the seafront to the Grand Hotel, which

was the only section of the Paignton route to be opened under the Dolter system. Unusually for a Tour, the car went clockwise round Babbacombe. According to the Rule Book, passengers were allowed a short walk along the cliffs:

On the return journey, if the majority of passengers desire it, a quarter-of-an-hour may be allowed to passengers to walk over Babbacombe Downs, the Conductor escorting them (after lifting the folding step and closing the rear platform-gate) from Babbacombe Downs Road to St. Annes Road via the Downs.
    The Car, in charge of the Motorman, must then proceed slowly to St. Annes Road and wait in the loop for the return of the passengers.

Like Brighton, Torquay's tourists travelled on top of the car, and again the conductor was under instructions to point out places of interest. Torquay, however, allowed normal passengers to ride inside the Tourist Car at ordinary fares. The driver was instructed to run as nearly as possible halfway between the normal service cars, whilst the poor conductor had to divide his time between giving his commentary upstairs, issuing tickets downstairs and preventing the lower orders from invading the top deck. If – as at Brighton – he passed the hat round at the end of the Tour, it would be hard to blame him.

End of the Dolter

The stud-contact system was no more successful in Torquay than in Hastings, and when the Tramways Company completed the coastal line to Paignton in 1911, they were allowed to use conventional overhead wires. The Town Council bowed to the inevitable, and the

THE TORQUAY ELECTRIC TRAMWAYS

rest of the system was converted during the same year.

With the Dolter out of the way, and the Paignton route open, the Company were able to extend the Tourist Cars along the coast, covering twelve miles – the longest tour in Britain, lasting 90 minutes and costing a shilling.

According to *Ward Lock's Guide* for 1912/13, Tourist Cars started from the Clock Tower at 11.00, 3.00, 4.30 and 6.15. A *Guide to Visitors* published by the Tramways Company (undated but probably pre-1915) shows morning, afternoon and evening Tours, but with multiple departures – at 10.30, 10.45, 11.00, 2.30, 2.45, 3.00, 6.00 and 6.15.

The 1917/18 *Ward Lock* includes the Tourist Cars but says only that "the times at which these Tours start are advertised", so perhaps wartime exigencies were making the operation less regular. The Tourist Cars were still listed in the 1924/25 *Ward Lock*, but probably ceased soon afterwards. It's likely that they suffered the same sort of motor-coach competition which defeated Brighton's Tourist cars, though the Torquay Company ran the coaches themselves, or through one of their subsidiaries.

Narrow-Gauge Leviathans

Since 1907 the Torquay Company had followed normal South Coast practice and operated nothing but orthodox four-wheel open-top cars. Then suddenly in 1923 they bought from the Brush Company two huge bogie cars, 36 ft. 8 ins. long - the largest trams ever built for a British narrow-gauge system. The only bigger specimens were home-made at Hartlepools by mounting two four-wheel bodies on one long underframe. Torquay managed to squeeze 76 seats into their new cars, which was still three less than Rothesay managed on their single-deck toastracks (*page 91*).

The two new cars were followed by two more in 1925 and a final pair in 1928. The arrival of these six cars had the effect of splitting the system into two - the Paignton route, worked primarily by the bogie cars from Preston Depot, and the Torquay town routes (including the Circular) run by four-wheelers from St. Marychurch.

A Notional Circular Tour

This division didn't stop the Tramways Company promoting a new Circular Tour in the Twenties - "Take the Circular Tour car. 11 miles. Fare 9d." This was misleading, to say the least, because Torquay didn't have a Circular Tour any more, and the journey could only be made by a change of cars, and

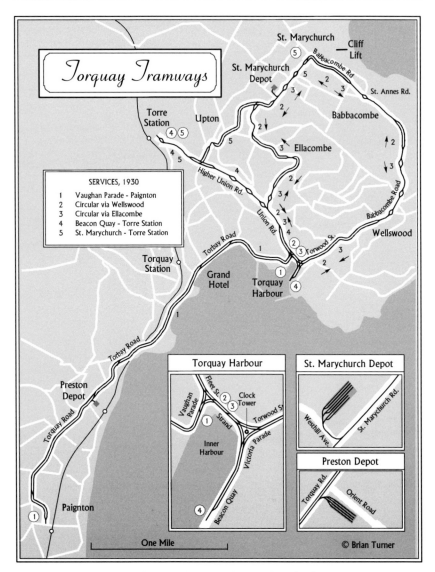

normal service cars at that. This purely notional tour had appeared in *Ward Lock* for 1920/21, which stated with rather more accuracy that "passengers may board the cars at any fare stage, and make a tour of eleven miles through Torquay, Paignton and Babbacombe back to their starting point, for 9d." The same edition

also mentioned a shorter tour at 4d., which must have been just a trip round the Circular route on the normal cars.

As far as is known, the 4d. and 9d. tickets lasted until the Torquay tramways were replaced within the space of seventeen days in January 1934 by Devon General buses.

Torquay's bogie cars, the largest narrow-gauge double-deckers in Britain, were confined to the Paignton route. In the centre window of No. 41 is an advertisement for the 9d. "Circular Tour".

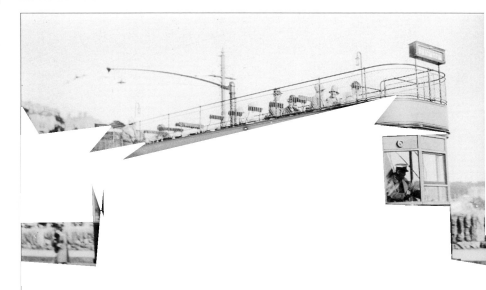

Four-legged Survivors (1)

By way of a change from the open-top four-wheelers which predominated on seaside electric tramways, a reminder that several British resorts never progressed beyond horse-cars, and some continued to run them even after the First World War. Douglas (IoM) still has them.

Morecambe, the most resolutely Luddite of them all, has Chapter Fourteen to itself, but these are two of the other horse-drawn systems; there are two more on page 104.

The Toast Rack, 5 Miles by the Sea, Sandgate, Seabrook & Hythe.

Above: The Sandgate & Hythe Tramway on the southern coast of Kent was unusual in being owned by a railway company - the South Eastern, who built toastrack No. 5 in their main workshops at Ashford in 1897. The line opened in 1891 and closed in September 1921, the penultimate English horse tramway, outlived only by Morecambe. No. 5 is standing at the eastern terminus at Sandgate, near Folkestone, about to set off along the coast to Hythe.

Below: If Morecambe was the horse-tram capital of England in the twentieth century, its Welsh equivalent was the tiny resort of Pwllheli, which had a population of only 3,700, but boasted two quite separate horse tramways. The Pwllheli Corporation Tramways, which ran for less than a mile from the railway station to the beach, had one of the narrowest gauges in Britain - only 2 ft. 6 ins. The line was run by three trams - two of them toastracks - and lasted from 1899 to 1919.

The other line was 3 ft. gauge and consisted of two routes. One ran from the station to the beach, further west than the Corporation line. The picture below shows an open car arriving at the beach terminus, where passengers could change for the line along the coast to Llanbedrog. The tramway ran from 1897 until the beach section was destroyed by the great storm of 28 October 1927. The section in Pwllheli ran for a few weeks in 1928 before the line closed completely - the last horse tramway outside the Isle of Man.

Above: **To judge from the photographs in this book, smiling for the camera is quite a recent convention. Before about 1930, most participants in group photographs seem to have maintained their dignity, but few managed to look quite so glum as this party from the Seamen's Mission climbing the steep hill from the Aquarium during a special tour round Scarborough's circular route. (SS)**

Below: **Perhaps the sombre seamen would have felt more at home on Scarborough No. 13, braving the North Sea near the Aquarium. (SS)**

Scarborough is reputed to have been the first seaside resort in Britain, which may be why in some respects – including its tramways – it resembled a South Coast resort more than a northern one.

The Scarborough Tramways Company opened its 3 ft. 6 ins. gauge tramway in 1904. The system was less than five miles long, but what it lacked in size it made up for in complexity, with numerous double-track junctions and a basic route that wasn't just a circular, but a figure of eight.

This Byzantine operation was worked by four nominally separate services. All the cars went right round the three-mile circuit, taking about 35 minutes. They carried boards advertising "Round-the-Town" at a fare of 3d. before the war, 4d. after, and 6d. from 1925.

The Grand Tour

Some time around 1908 the Tramways Company introduced a variation specifically for tourists. Exactly when it started isn't known, as the Scarborough tramways, like many company-owned systems, seems to have left few records

Above: **Scarborough's tramways were so quiet in winter that the crews had ample time to organise football matches. This is the Electric Tramways XI (or rather X) ready to take on the Electricity Supply Department.** *(SS)*

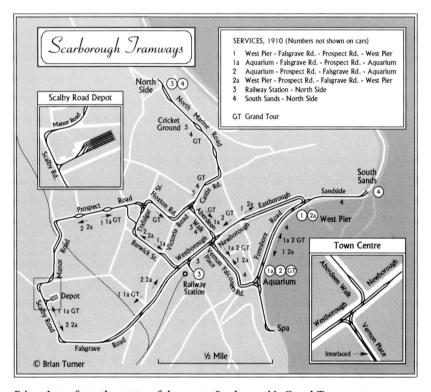

Below: **Away from the centre of the resort, Scarborough's Grand Tour route was mostly single track. This is Manor Road near the tram depot, with car No. 3 looking deceptively over-size against a largely juvenile entourage.** *(SS)*

behind it. Even the name of the operation is in doubt. Some sources call it the Grand Tour, but Ward Lock's guide to Scarborough says only that "special cars run, according to demand, designated Tour of the Tramways System", which doesn't have quite the same ring about it. This wording also appeared on the tickets for the Tour, which were bright red.

The Tour, whatever its name, started on the seafront at the Aquarium, and ran along the foreshore as far as the West Pier before doubling back up through the town, and following the figure-of-eight route round the western suburbs. Then it made a detour along a stretch of otherwise disused track in Hoxton Road, a narrow terraced street, to join the route to the North Side terminus. From there it retraced its steps before concluding with a hair-raising ride down a 1-in-10 hill back to the Aquarium.

The Tour cost 6d. for four miles and took a leisurely 75 minutes, including a walk in the Alexandra Gardens at North Side: it was never likely to be a quick run, with twelve junctions to negotiate en route. Passengers could board at any point on the circuit.

Problems

Scarborough's tramway system wasn't just complicated; it was also hilly and constricted by narrow roads and awkward track layouts. The town's trams were some of the smallest double-deck cars in Britain, open-top four-wheelers seating only 43 passengers. Today's visitors may well wonder how trams managed to negotiate Scarborough's streets at all.

Not surprisingly, this was the least successful of all Britain's seaside tramways, so reliant on visitors that it virtually closed down in winter. Indeed in October 1910 the Tramway Company shut up shop completely until the following April, despite a Court Order fining them 10s. 0d. for each day they failed to run the statutory service.

Wartime Demise

As if the Tramways Company didn't have problems enough, Scarborough was bombarded by the German Navy in December 1914, and nine residents killed. The visitors disappeared completely in 1915, and the Grand Tour with them.

This vulnerability to attack meant that Scarborough's tramways had very different wartime stresses from Blackpool or Brighton. In 1915, whilst Blackpool was earning over £6,000 from its Circular Tour alone, the total revenue from Scarborough's tram system came to only £2,854.

The Grand Tour never restarted after

the war, since the Company had lifted the track in Hoxton Road to use elsewhere. But the figure of eight, with its round-the-town fares, continued throughout the Twenties, whilst the undertaking itself staggered along unprofitably under various owners.

In the end the entire Scarborough system was replaced by buses on 30 September 1931 - the second seaside tramway to close, two years after Hastings.

Above left: **All is not quite what it seems. Scarborough never had toastrack trams, but the Tramways Company did operate runabout buses in the 1920s.** *(National Tramway Museum)*

Above right: **On a system with so many junctions, tram drivers had to be handy with the point iron. The driver of car 2 is leaning over the dash, changing the points outside the railway station to take him straight down Falsgrave Road and then back round the figure-of-eight. The board on the dash reads "Round the Town 6d."**

Below: **Scarborough 24's conductor contemplates a phalanx of competing buses blocking the track along the seafront by the Aquarium. Fortunately Scarborough's trams were only 6 ft. 3 ins. wide; better still, No. 24 had been bought second-hand from Ipswich, whose trams were six inches narrower. The advertisement on No. 24 reads "This Car Conveys You To & From The Passenger Steamers That Sail From The Lighthouse Pier".** *(SS)*

Last Days at Scarborough

Left: The atmosphere of the seaside tramway – with advertisements for concert parties - was still very strong in the final season of the Scarborough tramways. Car 24, bound for South Sands, passes No. 2 on the Circular route at West Pier in June 1931. *(A. Fellows/SS)*

Centre: The view from Scarborough railway station on the very last day, 30 September 1931, with the trams about to give up the unequal struggle against cars, motor-cycles, buses and charabancs. Ex-Ipswich No. 27 is on its way to North Side, whilst cars 5 and 28 are emerging from Westborough. *(SS)*

Bottom: Even after abandonment, trams remained part of the Scarborough holiday scene, serving as holiday accommodation at nearby Cayton Bay, along with a variety of old bus bodies.

Between 1905 and 1910 the most successful tourist routes in Britain were fairly small-scale operations on the hilly narrow-gauge tramways along the South and East Coasts – Brighton, Hastings, Torquay and Scarborough.

It wasn't until Blackpool introduced its toastracks in 1911 that a new dimension in tramcar tours opened up. The first resort to follow Blackpool's lead was Southport, just a short steamer trip away across the Ribble estuary. Indeed there were echoes of Blackpool, conscious or unconscious, in much that Southport did.

The Southport tramways were unusual for a holiday resort in that they didn't reach the sea-front - nor did the sea itself in later years - and that they were run by two operators. Southport Corporation owned the tram tracks within the borough but for many years leased them to the Southport Tramways Company.

The Southport system had been one of Britain's first small-town horse tramways when it opened in 1873. Its trunk route – electrified in 1901/02 – ran from Birkdale along the main boulevard, Lord Street, and then via two routes to the Botanic Gardens at the picturesque village of Churchtown.

With the introduction of electric

Southport pioneered the group photograph on the toastrack in 1915 – four years before Blackpool – though it doesn't seem to have lasted long. The location was the George Hotel in Duke Street. Southport, like Blackpool, employed women conductors during the war – by 1916 there were fourteen, six of them also trained as drivers.

traction (using municipal electricity) the Corporation decided to become tramway operators themselves. This was very much the vogue at the time, but in Southport's case it was a grave mistake. With the Company as sitting tenant, the Corporation had to develop a complete new tramway system of their own, serving the residential areas inland. They did this with great enthusiasm and during 1900 laid tracks in almost every street that was wide enough, and one or two that weren't.

Southport's "Marton Route"

In 1901, just like Blackpool, the Corporation completed a route which circumnavigated the town. Unlike the Marton route, Southport's "Inner Circle" was a complete circuit, but proved no more successful, and by 1910 was losing about £2,000 a year. Almost as problematical was the route along Scarisbrick New Road towards Kew Gardens, which was so unremunerative out of season that the winter service only ran as far as Haig Avenue.

One of the problems was the opening of new municipal attractions on the

Promenade to counter the disappearance of the sea, as the estuary silted up following the deepening of the channel to Preston Docks. Unfortunately these attractions only served to take business away from the Corporation's own tram routes. The Corporation had in fact obtained powers to lay a line along the Promenade, but unwisely linked them to a long-running proposal for a transporter bridge across the Ribble to connect the Southport tramways with the Lytham and Blackpool systems. When this scheme finally collapsed, the Corporation had lost heart and the powers expired in 1910.

By then the losses on the tramways were mounting year by year, and in 1912 the Corporation commissioned the Liverpool Tramways Manager, Charles Mallins, to investigate the system. Mallins recommended closing several stretches of track, including the Inner Circle.

This drastic proposal seems to have stimulated the Corporation into more positive action. Perhaps someone noticed the parallels with Blackpool's Marton route, and the way its fortunes had been revived by the Circular Tour.

A rare view of Southport Corporation's original Circular Tour via the Inner Circle route in 1914, with new toastrack 21 at the railway bridge in St. Luke's Road. The picture may have been posed, as the car is travelling clockwise round the route. *(GP)*

Southport began its adventure into Circular Tours in an even lower key than Blackpool had done in 1905. During the summer of 1913 they started selling a "Circular Tour" ticket which allowed two people to travel round the Inner Circle for 3d., saving a penny on the normal 2d. round trip fare.

The impact on Southport's visitors was hardly electric. Only 1,564 tickets were sold that year, but it was the first step towards emulating Blackpool's phenomenal success.

The First Toastrack

In October 1913 the Corporation took the second step, and decided to buy a toastrack from the United Electric Car Company at Preston, who had built the Blackpool cars. It wasn't a major investment - only £220, since the Corporation cannily decided to buy just the body and fit it to an existing four-wheel truck.

The new car arrived in March 1914, and was given the number 21. It was a smaller version of the Blackpool cars, with ten benches for 50 passengers, and was finished in the dark red Southport livery, very similar to the colours then in use at Liverpool. It had the same style of painted destination boards as at

Blackpool. On one side was "Circular Tour" which was used when the toastrack ran round the Inner Circle occasionally in 1914. The other side bore the stirring legend "Grand Tour".

The Grand Tour

The Grand Tour was the Corporation's riposte to Mallins' gloomy report. Like Blackpool, they were aiming to boost revenue on the loss-making Inner Circle and Kew Gardens routes, so they concocted a remarkable itinerary to cover both lines.

The Grand Tour started in London Square, just off Lord Street, and went anti-clockwise round the town. Tourist routes usually went anti-clockwise, since it was easier to turn left than right at junctions, and Southport had more than its share of those. The Corporation system also had an unusually high proportion of single track, often along very narrow streets.

To make the Tour as Grand as possible, the toastrack took the longest route out of town, following the Cemetery route via Duke Street. Then it turned left along Cemetery Road and Ash Street to reach Scarisbrick New Road, which led eastwards to Kew Gardens. Unfortunately there were no points turning east, so the toastrack had to run across the junction and shunt backwards into Scarisbrick New Road before heading out of town towards Kew Gardens.

At the Gardens the car had to reverse again, using Brighton's device of taking the passengers for a short walk in the park while the trolley and seats were turned. Back at Ash Street the toastrack once again had to run across the junction and then shunt backwards to regain the circular part of the route.

The next stretch, along St. Lukes Road and Hartwood Road to Manchester Road was, for long periods, used solely by Tour cars as the Inner Circle route ran only fitfully in later years. At Manchester Road the toastrack joined the Company's Roe Lane route and returned to town along Manchester Road and Lord Street.

The Grand Tour was 6½ miles long, and cost 6d. Locals were sceptical that anybody would pay so much for a tram ride, but they did. During its first two days - starting on Good Friday, 10 April 1914 - the new toastrack completed 24 circuits and earned over £16.

Never on Sunday

Like all the Corporation routes, the Grand Tour didn't run the next day, Easter Sunday - or any other Sunday - in deference to the powerful religious lobby

Southport Corporation, like Blackpool, published an official picture postcard of its Grand Tour, buying 25,000 cards for a modest £7. 7s. 6d. in June 1914. The car is No. 21 at the loading point in London Square, with Lord Street on the left. This version of the photograph is taken from the Corporation's 1915 Holiday Guide.

SOUTHPORT CORPORATION TRAMWAYS

GRAND TOUR

STARTING FROM LONDON SQUARE.   DISTANCE ABOUT 6 MILES.   TIME ABOUT 50 MINUTES.
ADULTS 6d.   CHILDREN 3d.

in Southport, which claimed to be the only town in England with more churches than pubs. In Blackpool, where God rarely got the better of Mammon, this battle had been fought and lost as early as 1896 – good news for the future Circular Tour, since Sunday was always its busiest day. As one councillor put it, "there's worse things going on in Blackpool on a Sunday than trams running". Sunday running at Southport didn't start until March 1918 after a long and bitterly-fought battle.

More Toastracks

The Grand Tour was soon earning 2s. 7d. per mile, three times Southport's normal revenue. Just as had happened at Blackpool, the solitary toastrack seemed to attract visitors like bees to a honey-pot, and Southport too had to draft in other cars to meet the demand. On Easter Monday there were four ordinary cars on the Tour, and on 20 May, a Scottish party needed seven plus the toastrack. The shunting which this convoy must have involved at Ash Street, right in the middle of the main road into town, beggars the imagination.

Only two weeks after No. 21 entered service, Southport ordered three more toastracks, again on old equipment, this time from withdrawn California cars. The order reached Preston at the same time as Blackpool's order for toastracks 87 – 92, and it's quite possible that the nine bodies were built together.

The three Southport cars were delivered towards the end of May 1914, and given the numbers 23, 25, and 27 under Southport's (literally) odd system of distinguishing single-deckers from double-deckers. The trucks and equipment were fitted in time for them to enter service during Whit weekend at the beginning of June.

Success

By July 1914 the Grand Tour was running twenty times a day and earning £400 a month. It was Blackpool all over again. Perhaps because Southport's toastracks were smaller and fewer, the passenger loadings were higher – 75% full in 1914 against 60% at Blackpool.

Southport was cannier with its fares, too, and wouldn't let passengers board en route. The sole concession was a 3d. child's ticket, but as only one passenger in six was a child, the average fare still worked out at 5½d. Each round trip on the Grand Tour took 17s. 0d. against 11s. 0d. on Blackpool's shorter route, so in the end honours were about even. The point is that both routes were highly lucrative.

Like Blackpool, Southport's Circular

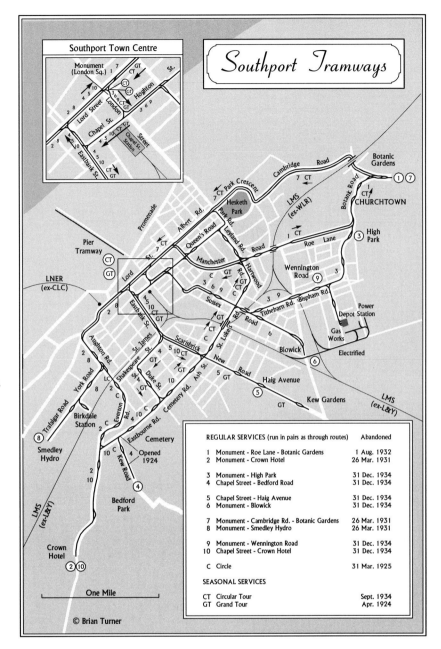

For the sake of clarity the Southport tram routes are shown above as individual services, each running from the town centre. In practice they operated as through routes, as shown in the inset. Trams showed the route number of their ultimate destination: a car leaving Smedley Hydro would display "7 – Botanic Gardens" and return showing "8 – Smedley Hydro".

Tour suffered only slightly from the First World War, though passenger figures fell sharply in 1918 when the fare was increased from 6d. to 9d. The child's fare doubled to 6d., which can't have helped. The Corporation perhaps had other things on their mind, having taken over the Southport Tramways Company in January 1918.

A New Circular Tour

Like Blackpool again, there was a postwar boom in Tour riding, peaking in 1920 when almost 130,000 passengers were carried. One of the reasons for this increase was the introduction in 1920 of

a new Circular Tour which covered some of the old Company routes.

Once again the Corporation found that, for all the plethora of junctions on the Southport system, there still wasn't enough pointwork for the new tour, so the Circular turned out to be almost as tortuous as the Grand Tour, requiring two reversals.

It followed much of the Grand Tour in Southport itself, without the detours along Duke Street or to Kew Gardens. Then at the point where the Grand Tour turned left into Manchester Road to head back to town, the Circular went straight across into Leyland Road, which

Southport's main tram route along the elegant boulevard of Lord Street was operated for 45 years by the Southport Tramways Company until the Corporation bought them out in 1918. This 1921 photograph shows one of the Company's original electric cars of 1901, newly top-covered by the Corporation.

wasn't used by any other service. There the passengers had to get off whilst the seats were reversed, and the toastrack then turned left into Manchester Road to go out via the old Company route along Roe Lane to the Botanic Gardens. The return to town was via the other Company route along Cambridge Road and back onto Lord Street.

Three More Toastracks

To run the Circular as well as the Grand Tour, the Corporation ordered three more toastracks in 1919 (Nos. 29, 31 and 33), again using second-hand equipment. The bodies, which arrived in June 1919,

were identical to the previous cars, but now cost £480 each. They were painted in Southport's new colours of bright red and primrose, with the trolley mast and destination box dark green, the same colour as the traction poles. The older toastracks received this livery at their next repaint, except that for some reason No. 21's destination box was always finished in varnished wood.

Decline

The two Tours ran together until early in the 1924 season when the Grand Tour was abandoned. This may have been because Kew Gardens was becoming

run-down or because increasing road traffic was making the shunting and reversal in the middle of Scarisbrick New Road unacceptable. The Circular Tour continued successfully; passenger figures dropped slightly during the Twenties, but not as severely as in Blackpool. In 1930 the receipts came to £1,049, which was nearly half Blackpool's figure for that year.

However there was no longer enough traffic to require seven cars, particularly as Southport, unlike Blackpool, didn't use the toastracks on their other routes. In December 1930 it was decided to dispose of "the three old toastracks now at the depot", though it seems that in fact only two disappeared.

Abandonment

In 1930 Southport Corporation decided to abandon their tramways over a ten-year period. First to go were the ex-Company lines to Birkdale and to Churchtown via Cambridge Road, which closed in March 1931. However the line to Churchtown via Manchester Road and Roe Lane was retained, and the Circular Tour was diverted there from Cambridge Road. The fare was reduced to 6d. to reflect the removal of part of the journey.

In 1932 the abandonment timetable was shortened. The next victim was the Roe Lane route, which closed on 1 August 1932, right at the height of the holiday season. It's believed that the tracks and wires in Roe Lane were left in

Potential Circular Tour passengers view the steps on Southport 23 with some trepidation at the Monument. *(N. Hamshere)*

place for the sole use of the Circular Tour until it stopped running at the end of the season.

The Tour never restarted in 1933, and the five surviving toastracks were sold for £119, presumably as scrap. The remaining routes all closed together on the last night of 1934 in a rather bizarre ceremony which started with the Transport Committee going to see a performance of "Jack in the Beanstalk" and ended with one of the last trams being set on fire outside the depot as some sort of sacrificial offering. At least Blackpool never thought of that.

Above: No. 29's conductor is keeping a look out for passengers as the car waits on the curve at the Monument in the early Twenties.

Below: For some reason the conductor is "trolleying" No. 29 as it moves off behind an open-balcony double-decker (either 24 or 28) on route 3.

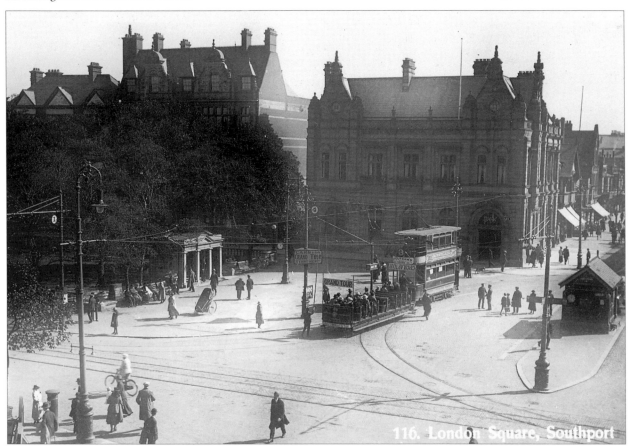

116. London Square, Southport

A Farewell Tour of Southport, July 1932

D r. Hugh Nicol – one of a handful of amateur photographers recording the disappearing seaside tramways of Britain in the early Thirties – visited Southport on 9 July 1932 for a final journey on the Circular Tour.

Top: Dr. Nicol boarded toastrack No. 31 at its usual loading point by the Monument, formerly London Square. A collapsed sewer in Leyland Road was playing havoc with the tram routes, and the toastracks had forsaken their traditional exit via Chapel Street, though it isn't certain exactly which way they went. This explains why the passengers are facing one way, and the trolley the other. It doesn't explain why the route board at the far end has been turned round.

Right: The sun came out as No. 31 left the Monument, in the opposite direction to normal. As soon as the car was back on Lord Street, the trolley was turned and placed on the northbound wire. No. 31 was actually running wrong line on the southbound track, because the sewer works necessitated a long stretch of single-line working. In front of No. 31 is a double-decker on Route 1, the truncated service to the Botanic Gardens. From 1873 until March 1931 this had been Southport's main tram route, running through to the Crown Hotel at Birkdale, but for its final sixteen months it ran only as far as the town centre, reversing in Lord Street, just north of the Monument. The passengers facing the camera are on the fixed seats either side of the trolley mast.

Below: At the Botanic Gardens, looking towards the terminus, toastrack 31 meets up with another Route 1 car, appropriately No. 1. The toastrack is now facing the other way, so it must have had at least one reversal on its journey from the town centre, but Southport's tour itineraries were so convoluted that it may even have had three. *(Dr. Hugh Nicol, National Tramway Museum)*

12. Round Southend's Boulevards

For a few heady weeks in the last pre-war summer of 1914, six British resorts were running tourist routes. The sixth – and last – to introduce one was Southend-on-Sea, whose tramway system was in some ways a mixture of the other five - narrow-gauge like Brighton, Torquay and Scarborough, but flat like Blackpool and Southport. Its Circular Tour was very much a mass-market operation, like those in the two Lancashire resorts.

The Southend system was similar in shape to the original Southport Company tramways, with a long, straight main line running through the resort from Leigh-on-Sea in the west to Southchurch in the east, following the coastline but several hundred yards inland behind the railway.

There was a short inland circular route to Prittlewell, and an even shorter branch from the Southchurch route down to the "Beach" terminus by the Kursaal, which was Southend's equivalent of Blackpool Pleasure Beach. This was as close as the trams came to the sea for seven years after the system opened in 1901.

The Boulevards

The impetus which eventually brought about Southend's Circular Tour came from a prominent local land-owner,

Colonel Burges. Just to the east of the town at Thorpe Bay he was developing a high-class suburb, aimed at well-to-do London commuters, who were served by a new station which the London Tilbury & Southend Railway built at the Colonel's expense in 1910.

No commercial activity was permitted on the estate, and residents were expected to travel into Southend by tram to do their shopping. The trams would be provided by extending the Southchurch and Beach routes through

Above: **Crossbench car 40 on the boulevards which made Southend's Circular Tour so attractive. No. 40 has just turned into Southchurch Boulevard at Bournes Green during the Tour's first summer in 1914. *(RD)***

Below: **No. 41 resting between trips at the Kursaal during the Tour's initial season. In the foreground is the booking office for the "toastracks" on the Tour, with an elaborate layout of loading barriers – the other extreme from Blackpool's free-for-all in Talbot Square.**

No. 41 at the Kursaal in 1914 again, but probably a little earlier, since this is the Tramway Committee's official journey round the new Circular Tour. Cars 40 – 42 were the last new design of crossbench car in the country. The livery was Southend's standard dark green, but changed after the war to a lighter green with a cream dash. *(RD)*

the estate to form a circular route.

The first extension from the Kursaal along the sea-front opened in August 1908, but since the work involved building a complete new esplanade, it took six more years for the entire circular route to materialise. The line along the esplanade was an orthodox street tramway, though the tracks were offset towards the sea side of the road. Through the estate, however, the tramway was laid as private sleeper track with roads on

one or both sides; these 100 ft. wide boulevards were planted with decorative trees and shrubs. It was a very advanced concept for its day. The last section of the new tramway had to wait until the bridge under the railway was rebuilt, but eventually the completed circle was opened to traffic on 16 July 1914.

The Circular Tour

The Corporation must have been acutely aware of the problems of circular tram

routes. Their own Prittlewell circular had been such a financial disaster that they abandoned half of it in 1912 and re-used the rails and overhead on the boulevards. They must also have seen how the introduction of tours had transformed the unremunerative Marton route at Blackpool and the Inner Circle at Southport.

Right from the start Southend intended to run a tour round the boulevards. In March 1914 they ordered

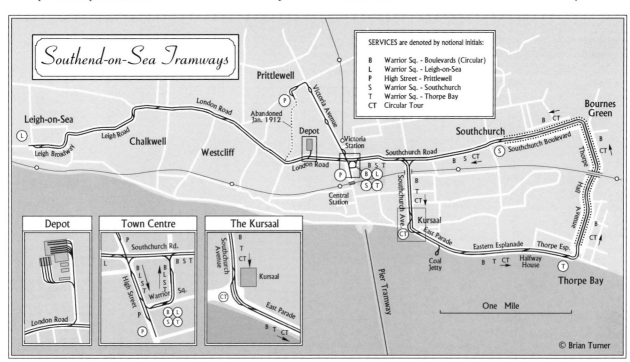

three crossbench cars from the Brush Company at Loughborough, with delivery timed to coincide with the completion of the circle. In the event the cars arrived a week late on 24 July, but the Circular Tour was able to start on 1 August, in time for the peak of the holiday season.

The Southend Tour was unusual in that it went nowhere near the town centre. However after the convoluted itineraries at Southport, Scarborough and Brighton, Southend's Circular Tour was simplicity itself – just a rectangle with a solitary junction to negotiate. It started from a siding on the Promenade near the Kursaal, and ran along the seafront to Thorpe Bay, then turned inland along the new boulevards, and back through Southchurch. The combination of seaside and tree-lined suburbia made it undoubtedly the most attractive of Britain's Circular Tours.

The last leg of the journey was down Southchurch Avenue back to the Kursaal. But there was a snag. Just as at Southport, the junctions hadn't been laid with a Circular Tour in mind, and there was no east-to-south curve from Southchurch Road into Southchurch Avenue. Nor was there room to lay one without buying land from an owner who was reluctant to sell.

Eventually a sum of £300 was agreed, and the curve was laid in 1915, but to enable the Tour to start in 1914 the Corporation installed a facing crossover just east of the junction. Tour cars could then switch onto the eastbound track, cross over the junction, swing the trolley and run down Southchurch Avenue to the Kursaal – with the passengers facing backwards.

Success

The Circular Tour was a great success in everything except its timing, which could scarcely have been worse. Just three days after the Tour was inaugurated, the First World War broke out. Nevertheless in the two months of August and September the Tour carried 22,838 passengers. Demand often exceeded

In 1914 Southend Corporation built a coal pier just east of the Kursaal, and in the following year introduced three freight cars to carry fuel directly from barges to the power station next to the tram depot. To allow cranes to unload the barges, the pier had no overhead wires, and power was fed to the trams through a long cable. On what appears, from the shadows and the fashions, to be a summer morning in 1914, the Tramways Department is taking advantage of the unused pier to store two of the crossbench cars. It isn't clear whether they stayed there overnight, or just during the day when business on the Circular Tour was slack. The coal trams finished in 1931, but the tracks on the pier are still there. In the distance is Southend's better known pier. *(RD)*

Above: Car 43 entering the Boulevard reservation on Thorpe Hall Avenue. The cost of the six gardeners employed by the Tramways Department on the Boulevard was charged to the tram route, which didn't do much for its profitability. *(RD)*

Below: Open-topper No. 39, running on the regular Boulevard Circular route but showing "Circular Tour" on its blind, has just turned onto Thorpe Esplanade from Thorpe Hall Avenue. *(BR)*

Above: The siding at the Kursaal extended along the full length of the curve from Southchurch Avenue onto the seafront. In 1937 it was moved further east when a roundabout was built at the junction. No. 41 is leaving the loading point in the late Twenties, with another Tour car entering the siding from Southchurch Avenue. *(RD)*

Below: Southend's Circular Tour followed the shore-line for a mile and a half from the Kursaal to Thorpe Bay. Only Blackpool gave its Tour passengers a comparable length of seafront for their money. Southend was one of the few narrow-gauge systems which were allowed to use enclosed double-deckers.

Below: Crossbench car 40, made redundant by falling demand for the Circular Tour during the Twenties, was rebuilt in 1929 as HMHS Carnival. This picture was taken at Leigh Church, the western end of the system and far removed from No. 40's old haunts. The driver's view was hardly panoramic. *(RD)*

supply, and the Corporation thought seriously about buying toastrack trailers to run behind the crossbench cars.

The war stubbornly refused to be "over by Christmas", and by the time the 1915 season arrived, Southend, like other holiday towns in this book, was moving onto a war footing. According to V.E. Burrows' history of the Southend Tramways, the Circular Tour only ran for the 1915 season and the crossbench cars were then converted into enclosed saloons for all-year use. However this now looks doubtful, as the traffic returns show income from the Circular Tour for each summer of the war. Perhaps just one of the three cars was converted.

Makeshift Circular Tours

During the first winter of the war, traffic on the new Boulevard route was so low that trams stopped running altogether after six o'clock. But as more and more troops were stationed between Thorpe Bay and Shoeburyness, demand for off-duty transport into Southend grew to the point where residents were being crowded off the Boulevard cars.

In 1916, therefore, an all-year circular service was introduced from the town centre, using ordinary cars which bore the destination "Circular Tour" - either to encourage pleasure riding, or because it was the closest suitable destination on the blinds. This produced a rather confusing situation with Tour cars displaying "Boulevard" while the regular cars showed "Circular Tour".

Postwar Revival

In 1919 the three "toastracks", as they were always known in Southend, carried 180,000 passengers and earned £4,130. In the league table of Circular Tour operators this put Southend second behind Blackpool's 565,000 (from 24 cars) and well ahead of Southport's 88,000. Brighton, who aimed for quality rather than quantity, chalked up a select 9,300 passengers, whilst Scarborough's Grand Tour never re-started after the war. Torquay's figures haven't survived, but would be nearer Brighton's than Blackpool's.

With demand exceeding supply again, Southend, like Southport, decided to expand their Circular Tour fleet in 1919, though only by a single car. While Southport managed to have their three new cars delivered within a few months, Southend had to wait two years. By the time the new car, No. 43, arrived in 1921, the Circular Tour was beginning to lose its appeal, and passengers had fallen to 134,000.

Slow Decline

Demand for the Tour stabilised for a few

years before starting a steady decline, though nowhere near as severe as at Blackpool. In 1929 Southend's three remaining cars carried 75,000 passengers, whilst Blackpool's thirty racks only managed 100,000 from the Circular Tour. To be fair, the Blackpool cars spent most of their time on Promenade

duties, whereas Southend, like Southport, didn't use its Tour cars on other routes.

By this time supply was exceeding demand, so in 1929 Southend withdrew crossbench car 40, and rebuilt it as "HMHS (His Majesty's Hospital Ship) Carnival" to raise funds for the local hospital. No. 40 only lasted in this guise

Above: **No. 43 loads on the new siding at the Kursaal on 24 August 1937, the Tour's last full season.** *(M.J. O'Connor, National Tramway Museum)*

Below: **Car 41 on the Boulevards not long before the Tour finished in July 1938.** *(W.A. Camwell, National Tramway Museum)*

This photograph is believed to show the final run of Southend's Circular Tour on 6 July 1938. The two cars are standing on the Tour siding in its relocated 1937 position along the seafront. (R. Sims/RD)

until 1932, when it was broken up. Being rebuilt as a boat became an occupational hazard for tourist cars: both Portsmouth and Blackpool did something similar.

Fares

One reason for Circular Tour traffic holding up so well during the Twenties was that, unlike other resorts, Southend never increased the fare beyond the pre-war level of 6d. But the slow downward trend was inexorable with the growth of motor-coach competition, and by 1933 traffic had fallen to 50,000. Halfway through the 1934 season the Corporation reduced the fare to 4d. - quite a bargain for a four-mile ride. Passenger figures for 1935 rose to 74,000, which unfortunately wasn't enough to prevent the revenue falling to £1,000. For the 1936 season the fare seems to have gone up marginally to 4½d.

Even when the fare was 6d. (and 3d. for a child) Southend's annual receipts from the Tour show some decidedly odd-looking totals - £3,379. 2s. 5d. in 1920, for instance. This may be just a case of "overs" and "shorts", or it may be, as Roy Anderson suggests in his history of Southend in *Tramway Review No. 40*, that the conductors issued "nearly-all-the-way tickets" of 4d. and 5d.

If they did, it seems to have been the only complication that Southend's conductors had to face. They didn't need to negotiate the running-board to issue tickets, since the fares were taken before leaving the Kursaal; in fact for many years, passengers bought their tickets at a kiosk. At one point the Corporation also apparently employed young boys to warn Tour passengers to keep their arms inside

the car along the boulevards. All in all, with only one junction to worry about, Southend's Tour drivers and conductors seem to have had a pretty easy time of it.

The End

During the Thirties, Southend - like Brighton and Blackpool - clung doggedly to their trams against the prevailing trend, even buying second-hand cars from Middlesbrough and Accrington. Since 1925, though, the Corporation had been gradually introducing trolleybuses. Southend was one of the few towns in Britain – along with Bradford and marginally Aberdare – which ran trolleybuses to supplement, rather than replace trams. At the beginning of 1937, the fleet consisted of seven motor buses, 21 trolleybuses and 53 trams, including crossbench cars 41 – 43 on the Circular Tour.

1937 was to be the last full season for Southend's Tour, but nobody realised this at the time, least of all the Corporation, who at the beginning of the year built a roundabout at the Kursaal, where the Tour still loaded on its special siding. Trolleybuses had been turning round there since 1929, and road traffic was making the junction with Southchurch Avenue very congested. The main tracks ran straight through the new roundabout, but the siding on the curve was replaced by a shorter one, two cars long, just east of the junction.

By the end of the 1937 season, the passenger total had fallen below 50,000 again, and the days of the Tour would surely have been numbered anyway, had not *force majeure* intervened. The problem was that the tracks along the boulevards had never been relaid since they were put down in 1914 – and some had been second-hand even then. Despite being patched up in 1936, their condition was now critical.

Faced with an expensive investment in relaying the Boulevard route, which had never been a goldmine, the Corporation opted to replace the trams by motor buses as soon as the licences could be obtained.

The licensing procedure was completed at the beginning of July 1938 and on the 6 July the Boulevard route was abandoned, and the Circular Tour with it. The three crossbench cars were kept for a while in the hope of finding a buyer. Llandudno was the obvious – indeed only – potential customer for narrow-gauge crossbench cars, but didn't want them and they were scrapped in 1939. The remains of the Southend system closed in April 1942.

Southend's three crossbench cars 41 - 43 sit hopefully in the depot, awaiting a buyer. None came; there never was a great demand for crossbench cars, even on standard-gauge systems. (J. Pullen)

13. A Toastrack Trio

Car No. 20, seen at the Giant's Causeway terminus in Northern Ireland, was arguably Britain's first electric toastrack (dating from 1899) though the benches were only open at one side. There were three of these open cars and a similar one with a light roof. Eventually all four had roofs, and three were later fitted with windscreens.

*S*outhend's track layout was almost as simple as a tramway could get and still run a Circular Tour. But several British seaside tramways were simpler still - just a single A-to-B route. Although none of these systems could run a tour as such, three of them did the next best thing and catered specifically for tourists by operating open cars.

The largest users of toastracks have already been mentioned - Blackpool with thirty, and Southport with seven. The remainder of this rare species ran on three small seaside tramways, each of them highly individual, but with several things in common - all narrow-gauge; all with a mixture of street and cross-country track; none of them in England.

Altogether the geography of the toastrack made little sense. Seaside tramways in the south and east of Britain, where the climate ought to have been more suitable, didn't favour toastracks, and only Southend and Weston-super-Mare had roofed crossbench cars. For no very obvious reason, the toastrack was a north-western creature, concentrated almost entirely in a ring around the Irish Sea.

Giant's Causeway

The first electric tramway to use open cars was the 3 ft. gauge roadside line from Portrush to the Giant's Causeway

in Ireland, which opened in September 1883, two years before the Blackpool Promenade tramway.

The original fleet consisted of two closed saloons, an open car (No. 3), a semi-open car (No. 4), and three toastrack trailers. No. 4 was similar to No. 3 but had a light roof. Both were cut-down versions of the saloons, with longitudinal seats and end platforms. Neither counted as true toastracks, though the trailers did: they were 18 feet

long, with six benches for 24 passengers.

Giant's Causeway No. 3 remained the solitary open motor car on the line for the next sixteen years, although the trailer fleet was augmented by five more toastracks built on the frames of redundant goods wagons - their riding qualities may not have been ideal.

In July 1899 the line was converted from third-rail current collection to overhead wires, and two more open cars were acquired. It seems that the bodies

The blind side of car 22 at Portrush station on 12 July 1935, with a typical all-purpose Giant's Causeway train, offering open, semi-open and closed accommodation. The "flag-pole" at each end of the car was for the conductor to hook down the trolley when the car was coasting, saving wear on the overhead wire. *(A.W. Houghton)*

Above: **An unusual view of a solo No. 22 rounding the corner into Eglinton Street on the last leg of its run to Portrush in the 1920s.**

Below: **Car 23 at the Giant's Causeway terminus. No. 23 always had a roof, and the other three cars were rebuilt similarly in 1936.**

Below: **The eastern terminus of the Rothesay tramways was at Guildford Square, right beside the harbour. A typically youthful Rothesay conductor is trolleying crossbench car 8 over the crossover. Car 7 is approaching the terminus while in the distance No. 10 heads out along the seafront on its way to Ettrick Bay, beyond the hills on the right.**

were built locally. Nos. 20 and 21 were a sort of semi-toastrack, with seven benches which were closed at one end since passengers always loaded from the road side of the line (the live rail was originally on the other side). A similar car, No. 22, arrived in 1902 and a roofed version, No. 23, in 1908. The original open car, No. 3, became a trailer.

Cars 20 – 23 ran the line for more than forty years, assisted from 1909 by a closed saloon car, No. 9, and later by a second-hand car acquired in 1937. After an accident in 1936 when a trolley fell off, the three open cars were rebuilt with roofs to match No. 23.

During the Second World War the tramway, which had run only in summer since 1925, reverted to all-year working, and cars 20, 21 and 23 were fitted with windscreens, the only examples of this configuration, since the Fleetwood Vanguards were scrapped in 1939.

The Giant's Causeway line closed on 30 September 1949. Throughout its long life its open cars were never quite 100% toastracks, but one way or another they came too close to be ignored completely.

Rothesay

From 1911 the Blackpool toastracks, with 69 seats, had the highest capacity of any British single-decker. But in July 1919 the Rothesay Tramways Company on the Isle of Bute put into service two enormous toastracks which seated ten more passengers.

The Company had opened a 4 ft. gauge horse tramway from Rothesay (described by the *Light Railway & Tramway Journal* as "the Margate of Glasgow") to Port Bannatyne in 1879, and electrified it in 1902, changing the gauge to 3 ft. 6 ins. In July 1905 they extended it across the island to Ettrick

To the Sands of Ettrick Bay

"This Car Runs Right Across the Island to the Sands of Ettrick Bay"

- Notice on Rothesay trams, 1930

Top: The crew take their ease on the front benches of Rothesay's home-built toastrack No. 11 at Guildford Square terminus, with row after row of empty seats stretching behind them. In the background is Rothesay harbour. The date is 8 September 1935, after No. 11 had been painted blue. *(D.L.G. Hunter)*

Centre: Britain's smallest toastrack was this tiny four-wheeler, No. 22, setting off across the island to Ettrick Bay in the mid-Twenties. The Rothesay Tramways converted No. 22 from an old one-man car in 1921/22. The conductor is David Rodger, aged about 13 and still in short trousers. His experiences as one of Rothesay's seasonal schoolboy conductors are recounted in Ian Cormack's history of the line.

Below: The photographer's Italian wife adds a touch of glamour to this view of Rothesay toastracks 11 and 12 inside Pointhouse Depot on 20 September 1930. Mrs. Nicol was reputedly adept at charming the staff at tram depots whilst her husband took photographs. *(Dr. Hugh Nicol, National Tramway Museum)*

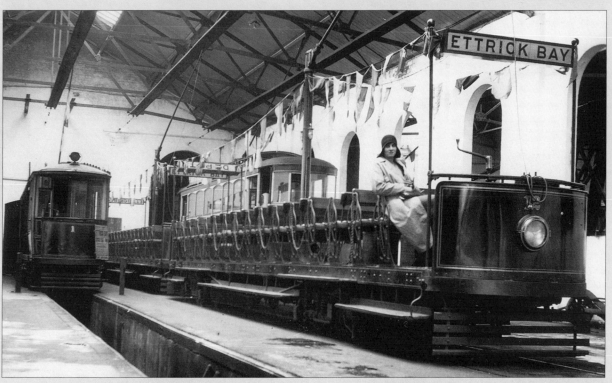

Rothesay's other terminus was a complete contrast, a bucolic spot on the west of the island at Ettrick Bay. Crossbench car No. 1 is having its front step lowered, and its trolley turned by one of Rothesay's conductresses – a rare breed which most other tramways only employed in wartime. For all the efforts of Reg and his Rhythm Band to drum up evening dance traffic to the Tramway's pavilion at Ettrick Bay, the writing is on the wall for the Rothesay trams, as one of the Company's new Albion buses speeds past. *(B.Y. Williams)*

They bought the parts for £350 a car, and paid a local firm £100 to assemble each toastrack at the tram depot. The cars were 42½ feet long, with 16 benches and seats for an astonishing 79 passengers. All this on the narrow gauge.

Not content with having the largest toastracks, Rothesay then built the smallest, No. 22, a 45-seater on the frame of an old one-man car which had come over the water from Greenock. It entered service some time in 1921 or 1922. This tiny four-wheeler bounced along Rothesay's sleeper track so exuberantly that on one occasion its conductor had to be taken off sick.

All three toastracks remained in service until the end of the 1936 season, when the Rothesay line was replaced by buses, some of them semi-open with centre-entrances, rather reminiscent of Blackpool, perhaps because their bodies were built there by Burlingham. The two large cars actually survived into early 1937 and were used in the dismantling of the line.

Llandudno & Colwyn Bay

The Llandudno & Colwyn Bay Electric Railway was in many ways the Welsh equivalent of Rothesay - a 3 ft. 6 ins. gauge line between two resorts, operated by long single-deck bogie cars.

So it's no surprise that Llandudno followed Rothesay's example and introduced toastracks in 1920. Unlike Rothesay, however, they bought them

Bay, giving a total length of just under five miles.

The Rothesay tram fleet reflected the line's dependence on tourist traffic. It consisted of ten long crossbench bogie cars (the third largest fleet in Britain after the Manx Electric Railway and the Fleetwood Tramroad) and ten similar

combination cars. So toastracks were a natural progression.

With typical island self-sufficiency, Rothesay decided to build their own toastracks, using bogies and electrical equipment from two cars whose bodies had been transferred to their associated tramway at Greenock on the mainland.

The Llandudno & Colwyn Bay line was one of Britain's most scenic tramways, but this was hardly reflected in its original fleet of fourteen completely enclosed bogie cars, including No. 3, which has just completed the eastern descent of the Little Orme at Penrhynside, around the time the line opened in 1907. It was 1920 before passengers could enjoy the scenery in the open air from four Preston-built toastracks. *(KG)*

A ticket from Llandudno's notional "Circular Tour", a round trip from any point on the line. (EO)

from Preston. The four cars were generally similar to the Blackpool cars, but longer and narrower.

The toastracks, Nos. 19 – 22, were part of a strategy to separate visitors from the local traffic in Llandudno. It worked: holiday-makers would often let the closed cars go by, and wait for a toastrack.

This wasn't the only example of Llandudno's initiative. Walter Hamilton, the line's manager from 1932 - perhaps having seen how Torquay had marketed a Circular Tour without actually running one - went one better that summer and devised a Tour on a straight A-to-B route. For a shilling, passengers could travel from any point on the line to one terminus, then to the other terminus, and back to wherever they boarded. This notional Circular Tour was advertised on the bumpers of the trams during the Thirties. It ceased in 1941, but was resurrected after the war, although no longer actively promoted.

The Llandudno cars eventually became the best-known of all electric

One of the Llandudno & Colwyn Bay Electric Railway's long bogie saloons stands at the original Colwyn Bay terminus whilst its crew watch a suffragette demonstration just before the First World War.

toastracks. They were the only operational examples to survive the Second World War, and preserve the experience of toastrack-riding for a postwar generation. Riding through Bodafon Fields and over the Little Orme on a toastrack was a formative experience for many a youthful tram enthusiast, including the author of this book

Sadly the Llandudno line and its fabulous trams fell just a few years short of a more perceptive age when they

would have been cherished as a national monument. The tramway closed on 24 March 1956 and, despite many requests, the four trams running on the last day didn't include a toastrack. In fact the last British toastrack tram had run on 25 September 1955. Unlike most of the "last runs" in this book, the British toastrack was at least given a proper farewell, as the final trip was a valedictory tour by the Light Railway Transport League.

The Llandudno & Colwyn Bay line didn't run along the seafront in either of its two terminal towns, but it did at the quiet intermediate resort of Rhos-on-Sea. Toastrack No. 20, with the usual flotilla of motor cars in attendance on 1 September 1953, is about to turn right onto the Caley Promenade and then head inland towards the A55 and Colwyn Bay. (H.B. Priestley, National Tramway Museum)

The Last Day of the British Toastrack

Above: After the Blackpool toastracks were withdrawn in 1942, the four cars at Llandudno soldiered on alone for another thirteen years. By the time they made their final runs on 25 September 1955, rather more people were interested than the handful of tram enthusiasts who had followed events before the war. This is No. 19 on a last-day tour, heading for the West Shore terminus on Llandudno's elegant Gloddaeth Avenue. *(David Packer)*

Below: Special Car – the final run by a British toastrack. The conductor folds the steps for the last time as Llandudno 22 prepares to leave the depot at Rhos-on-Sea for a farewell tour by the Light Railway Transport League. At least the sun shone for the occasion; it would hardly have been right to say goodbye to the toastrack in the rain. *(Richard Wiseman)*

14. Morecambe : Horse-tram Capital of England

THE TOWER, MORECA[MBE]

Morecambe, third of the great Lancashire resorts which grew from tiny villages during Queen Victoria's reign, never had a tourist tram service. It did have toastracks, though not electric ones. In fact it never had electric trams of any sort, but the trams it had were a tourist attraction in themselves. In the twentieth century, Morecambe was the undisputed horse-tram capital of England, with three operators running horse-cars long after they had disappeared from most of Britain's other towns and cities.

The horse-trams at Morecambe were nearly as late to start as they were to finish. The first section was opened by the Morecambe Tramways Company in June 1887, making it one of the last new horse tramways in the country. The line was gradually extended until it ran from the Strawberry Gardens at Heysham for

Above: **Morecambe horse-car No. 2 passing the short (and short-lived) Tower around 1910. The Tower was intended to be 232 ft. high, but work stopped at the 154 ft. level. It opened in July 1909, and was demolished in 1915. *(JDR)***

Below: **An Edwardian holiday-maker lifts his young daughter onto Battery-bound Morecambe car No. 10, whose driver looks round for a signal to start - in vain, since the conductor is upstairs collecting fares.**

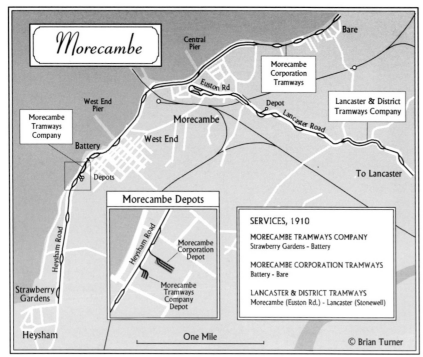

three miles northwards to Bare.

The Second Horse Tramway

The line along the seafront wasn't the only horse tramway in Morecambe. The Lancaster & District Tramways Company, which started even later – in 1890 – ran a four mile single-track route along the winding main road to Lancaster. The tracks came within a hundred yards of the other tramways in both Morecambe and Lancaster, but were never connected to either.

Although not strictly a seaside tramway, the Lancaster line was quite tourist-oriented. It was operated in its later years by some unusual open "observation cars" converted from double-deckers, before it died a very long-drawn-out death, eventually closing on 31 December 1921.

The Third Horse Tramway

Two horse tramways in one town might have seemed enough – particularly by 1909 when horse-trams only survived in a handful of other places. But that year Morecambe effectively acquired a third, when the Corporation took over the 2½ miles of horse tramway within the

borough, and began its own operation.

This left the Morecambe Tramways Company with the 1¼-mile rump within the Heysham boundary, from the Battery to the Strawberry Gardens. The tracks remained connected because the Corporation tram depot was on the Company section of the line, but there was no through running.

The Petrol Cars

From 1909 to 1911 the Morecambe Tramways Company ran the dismembered route to Heysham with three of their original horse-cars. The line was too short to justify electrification, so the Company invested some of the £13,000 proceeds of the sale on relaying their track and replacing the horse-cars (which they sold to the Corporation) by three new petrol-engined single-deckers – spiritual descendants of the old Lytham gas trams.

Leyland Motors built the "chassis" of the new cars and UEC the 36-seat bodies; altogether they cost £1,050 each. One axle was driven directly from the engine, which was on the platform at the Heysham end of the car, and the other was connected by chains. There was a water tank under the northern platform, and a radiator on the front of each dash.

The first car arrived by rail on 12 December 1911. Service began on 15 January 1912, when No. 1 made a run over the two systems – the first and last time a tram ran from Heysham to Bare after 1909. The other two cars entered service on 28 May 1912. The final car, No. 4, which arrived for the 1913 season, was completely open, but was a

The Lancaster & District Tramways Company's undulating four-mile route between Morecambe and Lancaster was operated in summer by single-deck "observation cars" cut-down from double-deckers, with raised floors to give passengers a view forward unobstructed by the hind-quarters of the motive power. This is the Lancaster terminus at Stonewell. The Dalton Square terminus of the Lancaster Corporation Tramways was only a hundred yards up Great John Street in the background. *(LCM)*

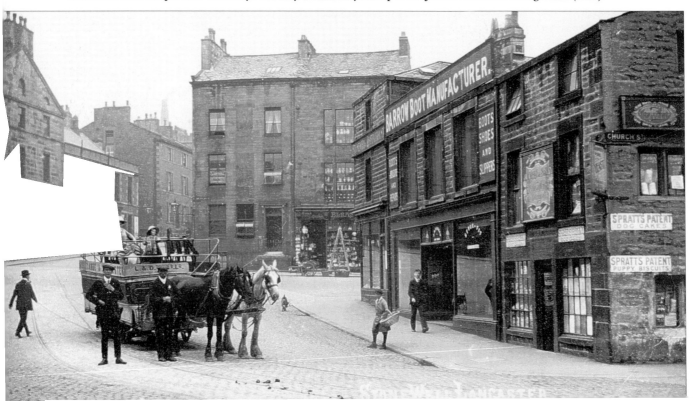

Above: News of coal strikes didn't bother the Morecambe Tramways Company's petrol car No. 1, seen when new at the Battery. The driver sat to the left of the engine; he had a foot brake as well as the normal tramcar hand brake. The photographer has co-opted some by-standers as "passengers", including Arthur Reed, the local barber, and his assistant, still in their white coats. (JDR)

Right: The only known view of open petrol car 4 in service, with its passengers about to transfer to Corporation horse-car 12 at the Battery.

Below: It wasn't easy to produce an impressive decorated car without electricity, but Morecambe Corporation did their best for the September Carnival.

cut-down saloon rather than a toastrack.

The petrol cars proved a good investment, and lasted until the tramway closed on 24 October 1924.

The Corporation Tramways

Morecambe Corporation continued to run its horse trams, despite numerous proposals for electrifying them. When the older trams acquired from the Company wore out, they replaced them with four brand-new horse-cars built at Strand Road – two toastracks in 1919 and two traditional double-deckers in 1922, appeasing the critics by saying that the toastracks could easily be converted to electric cars.

At that stage the Corporation showed every intention of keeping their horsecars indefinitely. In 1922 they built new stables and even planned to extend the line northwards. But a few years later they changed their mind, and the last horse tramway in England was replaced by motor buses on 6 October 1926.

Top: Twentieth-century photographs of horse-trams usually show them down-at-heel, and sagging from the combined effects of braking strains and anno domini. The four-square appearance of Morecambe 16 at the Battery is explained by the fact that the car is brand-new. It was one of two bought from English Electric at Preston in 1922 – the last new horse trams in England. (JDR)

Left: Morecambe Corporation finally grew weary of their tramway being a figure of fun on picture postcards, and abandoned their plans for retaining and extending the line.

Below: The end came on 6 October 1926. No. 16 had run for only five seasons. This valedictory postcard shows it with car No 9.

So far this Circular Tour of Britain's coastal resorts has looked at seaside tramways with regular tourist operations or toastrack cars. There were other resorts with rather less permanent facilities for tourists, and some with none at all.

Since most of these marginal seaside tramways were in the South of England, perhaps the best way to look at them is to set off down the East Coast from Scarborough, then along the English Channel until the seaside tramways run out at Weston-super-Mare.

Cleethorpes (Grimsby)

Cleethorpes barely qualifies as a seaside tramway at all, since for much of its life it was served from next door by the Great Grimsby Street Tramways Company. However in 1922 the Company introduced a tourist service with an open "Tram Coach" which they built themselves on an old four-wheel truck.

As its name suggests, Grimsby No. 40 was more akin to a motor coach than a toastrack, with a central gangway and rear entrance. It ran from the seafront at Cleethorpes to People's Park in Grimsby and back for 6d. Passengers could break the journey at People's Park, but then had to return by ordinary service car.

Above: One of the most appealing of all Britain's seaside lines was the 3 ft. 6 ins. gauge tramway at Weston-super-Mare – a perfect miniature of a system, with three single-track routes, each about a mile long, radiating north and south along the seafront and east to the tram depot. This is car 7 at Madeira Cove on the northern route, about to climb over the headland to the Old Pier terminus. Another double-decker can just be seen waiting at the next passing loop round the Cove. Weston had eight of these open-toppers, plus six four-wheel crossbench single-deckers.

Below: The Grimsby Tram Coach ran between Grimsby and Cleethorpes from 1922 to 1924. It isn't immediately apparent from this posed picture that the seats, upholstered in leather, were back-to-back. The extremely long overhang proved to be the Tram Coach's downfall when it ran over the complex and constricted tramways in Portsmouth after being transferred to the associated Portsdown & Horndean line in 1925.

Great Yarmouth car 6 at the Market Place on the northern half of the system. The tram service on the Fish Wharf route is recorded as being every ten minutes in winter with extra cars in summer and during the herring season; herrings must have been out of season when this picture was taken around 1920. The Fish Wharf route was one of the first seaside casualties, being converted to buses in May 1924.

It's unlikely that the Portsdown management were overjoyed at inheriting Grimsby's cast-off Tram Coach, which they numbered 17, but they ran it through to Southsea during the 1925 season. It may just have encountered Portsmouth Corporation's own reclusive toastrack during its travels.

Unfortunately the Portsmouth authorities took exception to the Tram Coach's long overhang - its 31 ft. body was mounted on a short 6 ft. truck - and banned it from the streets after the first year. It seems to have been scrapped soon afterwards.

Great Yarmouth

There were no more seaside tramways in Lincolnshire or Norfolk until Great Yarmouth, whose 3 ft. 6 ins. gauge system was longer than either Southend's or Brighton's. However it suffered from the fact that the River Yare divided the system into two physically separate sections (the opening bridge across the river was unsuitable for trams). The northern section served the main Promenade, but there was little scope for a tour, and seemingly no inclination at all to run open cars.

The fleet was a typical one of open-top four-wheelers, which didn't change from the last new car arriving in 1907 to the system closing in 1933.

Ramsgate and Margate

Skipping past the Thames Estuary and Southend, the next two holiday resorts with trams were Ramsgate and Margate, which were served by the Isle of Thanet system. One of the earliest seaside electric tramways, it never developed beyond an A-to-B route, though the line itself was an attractive mixture of seaside and country sections. There seemed no

The problem of turning the seats was avoided, if not solved, by having fixed seats facing each other in pairs, so that half the passengers travelled backwards. At least they travelled backwards in comfort, as the seats were upholstered in leather. If it rained, the Tram Coach had to scuttle back to the depot. In its first year No. 40 carried 3,534 passengers, rising to 5,649 and then 9,055 in 1924, its last year of operation.

In 1925 Grimsby Corporation took over the tramway within the borough and just before the take-over, the Tram Coach was re-gauged to 4 ft. 7¾ ins. and transferred to the Portsdown & Horndean Light Railway in Hampshire, which belonged to the same parent company. The roadside tramway which connected the two villages had running powers over the Portsmouth tramways to Southsea pier.

Isle of Thanet car No. 43 stands at the edge of Ramsgate harbour on a siding which was used by a short-working service to Broadstairs. The Thanet system was unusual in that all its cars had windscreens - those on No. 43 were home-made. *(BR)*

The only known photograph of Southampton's toastrack, seen at the Clock Tower when new in April 1916. No. 2 was virtually identical to the cars at Southport, except that it had an outside-sprung trolley.

Resort	Gauge	Cars	Miles	Electrified	Closed
	Seaside Electric Tramways				
Blackpool	S	208	20.45	29.9.1885	---------
Bournemouth	N	132	21.95	6.4.1901	8.4.1936
Brighton	N	80	9.46	25.11.1901	30.8.1939
Great Yarmouth	N	35	9.94	19.6.1902	14.12.1933
Hastings	N	65	19.37	31.7.1905	13.3.1929
Llandudno	N	24	6.52	19.10.1907	24.3.1956
Lytham St. Annes	S	55	6.31	28.5.1903	28.4.1937
Rothesay	N	22	4.87	19.8.1902	30.9.1936
Scarborough	N	28	4.78	6.5.1904	30.9.1931
Southend	N	57	9.22	19.7.1901	8.4.1942
Southport	S	45	17.40	18.7.1900	31.12.1934
Thanet	N	60	10.84	4.4.1901	24.3.1937
Torquay	N	42	9.24	4.4.1907	31.1.1934
Weston-super-Mare	S	16	2.92	12.5.1902	17.4.1937

This table excludes resorts which were served by adjoining ports, as well as tramways in the Isle of Man and Ireland. Cars and route-miles are the maximum ever operated; the figures for Blackpool, Bournemouth and Southport are after the municipalities there had absorbed the adjacent company tramways.

S = Standard gauge (4 ft. 8½ ins.) : **N** = Narrow gauge (3 ft. 6 ins.)

obvious impediment to toastracks or crossbench cars and the likeliest explanation for Thanet never using them is that they already had too many trams. By 1903 they had sixty cars, and never bought another one.

Southampton

Sailing by Hastings and Brighton on the South Coast, the tramways of Southampton were just about visible from the sea, though the town had no pretensions to be a seaside resort. All the more curious, then, that Southampton operated the only toastrack south of the River Mersey. Doubly curious that they built it during the First World War, when most tramways were struggling just to keep their existing cars on the road.

In 1916 Southampton's Tramways Manager, W.T. Robson, persuaded his Committee to rebuild an old double-decker into a single-deck toastrack to provide what *Tramway & Railway World* described as an "economical method of meeting periods of traffic rushes on holidays and special occasions". He estimated the cost at £50, which must have been optimistic in the extreme.

The job was done in Southampton's own works, using the underframe and equipment of car 2, and keeping its number. Most of the body parts came from the car works at Preston, and No. 2 was almost identical to the 50-seat toastracks supplied to Southport in 1914. It entered service on 20 April 1916, but doesn't appear to have had a dedicated route, and before long was down-graded to fairly mundane duties.

Southampton soon tired of their

solitary toastrack, and must have been delighted to sell it in May 1919 for a reputed £550, a remarkable figure even in the postwar seller's market for second-hand trams.

Portsmouth

The buyer for Southampton's unwanted toastrack was Portsmouth Corporation, who purchased it for a short-lived tourist service round the town.

Short-documented, too, because the only mention of it comes in S.E. Harrison's *Tramways of Portsmouth*, which records that "after minor alterations and repainting in Portsmouth's crimson lake livery with the fleet number of 104, it was used during Portsmouth's Peace celebrations in June and July 1919. In the following summer season, the toastrack made a Round Tour of Portsmouth for a fare of one shilling. As such, however, it

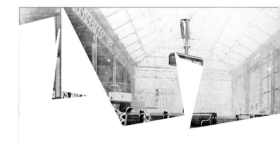

Above: No. 104 in Portsmouth's North End depot, soon after its transfer from Southampton. *(National Tramway Museum)*

Below: 104's third manifestation came in the late Twenties, when it appeared with this stylish roof, making it strictly a crossbench car rather than a toastrack.

Night photographs of trams with people on board are rare. This picture of Portsmouth 104 is doubly unusual because the passengers include some of the fastest men in the world - sea-plane pilots taking part in the celebrated Schneider Trophy races on the Solent in September 1929, and easily distinguishable from the pallid natives of Portsmouth.

was not a paying proposition, the wind resistance being too great to please many passengers." Which sounds a bit unconvincing for a town with a long naval tradition and a large fleet of open-top trams.

The next photographs of 104 show it as a crossbench car with a rather elegant roof, which was added in the Twenties. In this guise it occasionally featured as an illuminated car. In 1933 No. 104 was converted to a full-time feature car, with a boat-shaped body. The Portsmouth tramways were replaced by trolleybuses between 1934 and 1936, and No. 104 was scrapped during this period, but just when isn't certain.

Bournemouth's Luxury Tram

Bournemouth Corporation didn't have a tourist operation in the normal sense, but went one better by having a luxurious private-hire tram, appropriately No. 1 in the fleet. The town council originally bought the tram for their own use – the tramway equivalent of the Directors' Saloon, which was once common on Britain's railways.

They ordered it from George F. Milnes & Co. of Birkenhead. Before delivering it, Milnes took the opportunity to display No. 1 at the 1902 Tramways Exhibition in London, where it created something of a sensation. Nothing like it had been seen before (or since); it was the closest any British tramway ever came to the extravagant tourist cars favoured by American operators before the First World War.

This is how the exhibition catalogue described the car: "The interior walls are entirely of Chippendale mahogany, with beautifully carved mouldings. The ceiling is hung with Lunesdale tapestry and the floor is covered with rich crimson Wilton carpet. The windows are richly draped to match the rest of the upholstery and fitted with blinds of crimson Tammie, and handsomely-upholstered basket chairs are provided for twelve persons. Four mahogany tables are provided, and a buffet is fitted in one

Bournemouth's luxury single-decker No. 1 brightens up a rainy day with a private party of ladies on board and a dignified white-gloved driver.

corner. The car is brilliantly lit by electroliers of antique bronze."

Somebody soon decided that this gorgeous creation was too good – or too expensive – to sit in the tram depot awaiting the pleasure of the Council, and the car was made available for private hire. The charge for a return journey, with twelve passengers, was a guinea – much more refined than a simple £1.

No. 1 served this purpose until 1920, when it was down-graded slightly and its wicker chairs replaced by orthodox longitudinal wooden seats so that it could be used in normal service. When the Bournemouth trams were replaced by trolleybuses in 1936, No. 1's body – still with drapes at its windows – was used as a shelter at the terminus of the Iford trolleybus route. The body, though not the curtains, survived until the 1950s. A few more years and Britain's most opulent tramcar would surely have been preserved for posterity.

Weston-super-Mare

Weston-super-Mare had one of the most delightful of all seaside tramways – a tiny gem of a system, with three single-track routes radiating north, south and east from the town centre, each of them only about a mile long. Weston was one of a cluster of tramways around the Bristol Channel which used standard gauge rather than the 3 ft. 6 ins. adopted nearly everywhere else in southern England.

Like Scarborough, the Weston trams virtually closed down in winter, with just a single car covering all three routes, and then only between 12 o'clock and 6 o'clock. In summer, though, things could get hectic, particularly when a steamer arrived at the Grand Pier, and trams would run in pairs along the single track between the passing loops.

The basic fleet consisted of eight red and white open-toppers, but what really gave the Weston fleet its seaside appeal was a batch of four crossbench cars built by Brush for the opening of the system in 1902. They were the only crossbench cars in the South until Southend's three arrived in 1914. In 1927 Weston bought two more, which were by a long way the last new crossbench cars in Britain.

A three-mile single-track system didn't offer much scope for a circular tour or a tourist ticket, and Weston had neither. But otherwise it remained a perfect miniature of a seaside tramway until it closed on 17 April 1937.

The End of the Seaside Tram

The spring of 1937 was not a happy time for the lover of the seaside tram. Half the systems which were running the previous summer - Rothesay, Thanet, Weston

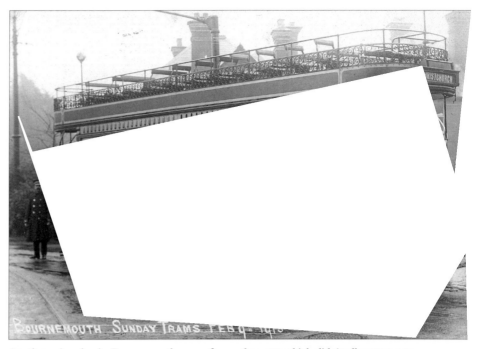

Another rainy day in Bournemouth, one of several resorts which didn't allow trams to run on Sundays; others insisted on a late start on Sunday mornings. Bournemouth eventually relented in February 1913, though it isn't clear whether this solemn group is celebrating or mourning the first Tram Sunday. Southport capitulated likewise in March 1918, but Rothesay held out until July 1925, and Colwyn Bay council were still fighting a rearguard action against the Llandudno & Colwyn Bay line in September that year. As it happened, Llandudno bought ten open-top bogie cars like No. 79 when Bournemouth closed in 1936, and ran them until 1956. (BR)

and Lytham - had closed, the last three within the space of five weeks.

Only Blackpool, Brighton, Llandudno and Southend remained. Happily none of the four showed much inclination to abandon their trams. Brighton and Blackpool were still putting new trams in service, and Llandudno and Southend had been buying second-hand.

In the event, however, Brighton and Southend folded up quite quickly, leaving only Llandudno and Blackpool to carry the flag of seaside pleasure riding rather uncertainly into the postwar world. Soon there was only Blackpool left, and things were just about back where they started.

Although Weston-super-Mare had the smallest tram fleet of any resort, it was the largest operator of four-wheeled crossbench single-deckers in Britain, buying four in 1902 and two more in 1927. No. 17, seen at the Grand Pier on 20 May 1929, was one of the last two crossbench cars built in Britain.

Four-legged Survivors (2)

Above: This most basic of crossbench horse-cars belonged to Arthur MacDougall, originator of the famous self-raising flour. It ran from 1898 to 1916 on the narrowest of all narrow-gauge tramways - 2 ft. gauge - which connected MacDougall's projected holiday resort at Fairbourne in North Wales with the ferry across the bay to Barmouth. There were two of these cars, seating seventeen passengers plus the driver. The Fairbourne line still survives, though getting even narrower as it gets older. In 1916 it was converted into a 15-inch gauge miniature railway, and rebuilt again to 12¼-inch gauge in 1986. *(KG)*

Below: Looking uncannily like some of the trams at Pwllheli, this is open car 19 taking some very stylish lady passengers along Causewayhead Road on the 3½-mile line from Stirling to the small Scottish spa resort at Bridge of Allan. Although not a seaside operation, this was very much a tourist line, with a sparse winter service and a varied fleet of summer vehicles - two "low cars" like No. 19, three toastracks and two crossbench cars - plus eight double-deckers bought second-hand from Edinburgh. It's thought that No. 19 was itself cut down from an Edinburgh double-decker around 1900. The Stirling line opened as early as 1874, and in its later years, like Morecambe, experimented with petrol traction to avoid the expense of electrification, but eventually closed in 1920.

PART 3. TOURIST VEHICLES

16. The Blackpool Toastracks

Chapter One told how, in August 1911, the fortunes of Blackpool's Circular Tour were transformed almost overnight by the arrival of the first toastracks. It was as though the whole concept of touring by tram had been waiting for the toastrack to be invented.

Not that anybody did "invent" the toastrack, since there was really nothing to be invented. The appeal lay rather in what was missing - no sides, no roof, hardly any ends. Somehow this minimalist approach seemed to strike an immediate chord with Blackpool's visitors. Perhaps it was the feeling of riding round town on a moving stage which appealed, especially to the ladies who could display their finery for all to see.

Cars 69 and 70 (1911)

The two toastracks which the Corporation ordered from the United Electric Car Company at Preston in April 1911 were basically a cut-down version of three crossbench cars, known as

Above: **The first of Blackpool's toastracks poses at Beechfield Avenue on Whitegate Drive, soon after being delivered in August 1911.** *(BL)*

"Vanguards", which the Fleetwood Tramroad had bought in July 1910.

The toastracks were fitted with the so-called Preston bogies which had first appeared under the Vanguards and were to become standard for both the Corporation and the Fleetwood Tramroad cars until 1933. In fact "Blackpool bogies" would have been more appropriate, since hardly anybody else used them.

There was no need for anything innovative about the toastracks' electrical equipment, which consisted of run-of-the-mill BTH B18 controllers and the traditional, indeed obsolete, 28 h.p. GE54 motors which had served Blackpool since 1902. The toastracks were the last new trams in Britain with these motors. Presumably they were the cheapest option.

It didn't take UEC long to build a toastrack, particularly as Blackpool did

the final assembly work. No. 69 entered service on 7 August and No. 70 a few days later.

Cars 71 - 76 (1912)

After the phenomenal success of the first two toastracks, the Corporation ordered another six in November 1911 at a cost of £552 each, for delivery in time for Easter 1912. Charles Furness said they would have ordered more, but there was nowhere to put them.

The first car arrived on 9 March, and all six were ready for Good Friday, 5 April 1912. As it turned out, Easter was a disappointment, with poor weather and a coal strike, and most of the new toastracks were back in the depot by Friday lunchtime.

The new cars were almost identical to Nos. 69 and 70, the only discernible difference being the "Blackpool Corporation Tramways" lettering on the

The second toastrack, No. 70, was also taken out for the photographer. No. 70 was fitted for a short time with these decidedly unsatisfactory cloth banners, illuminated by a string of clear bulbs. *(AMM)*

running board instead of "B.C.T." and a metal notice on the trolley mast. The wording, with its suggestion of dark deeds afoot, became compulsive reading for Circular Tourists: "Passengers are particularly requested to refuse any Ticket not punched in their presence or not bearing the full value of the Fare paid and to destroy their Tickets on alighting from the car."

Cars 77 – 80 (1912)

At the beginning of June 1912, the

Tramways Committee ordered another four toastracks. The first vehicle arrived on 22 July, and all were in service by 14 August.

They looked much the same as cars 69 – 76, except that they had nickel-silver handles, to save time cleaning the brass. Three of the cars had electrical equipment salvaged from recently-withdrawn conduit cars, and cost only £350 each, compared to £580 for the other car which was completely new.

The growing toastrack fleet was

absorbing depot space faster than the (substantially smaller) conduit cars were releasing it. An extension to Marton Depot was being planned, but in October 1912, as a rather desperate interim measure, the Corporation laid a temporary siding, running out of the south end of Blundell Street depot and part of the way along Rigby Road.

Cars 81 – 86 (1913)

With the Circular Tour still booming, the Committee ordered six more toastracks in December 1912. There was no rush for delivery, since there was nowhere to put the cars until the extension to Marton Depot was completed in the spring of 1913. They eventually arrived in June and July. The stock of old equipment was exhausted, so all six cars were completely new, costing £575 each.

Cars 87 – 92 (1914)

1913 was the high point of the Circular Tour, and at busy times there still weren't sufficient cars to meet the demand. Some members of the Council felt that there were enough toastracks already and that orthodox cars would be a better buy, but Furness argued that the queues in Talbot Square could only be cleared by toastracks, which were much quicker to load.

The Tramways Committee agreed,

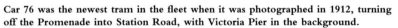

Car 76 was the newest tram in the fleet when it was photographed in 1912, turning off the Promenade into Station Road, with Victoria Pier in the background.

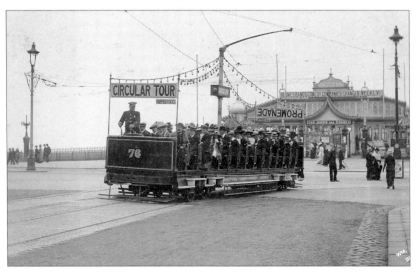

The toastracks were given headlamps in 1921. This is No. 72 soon afterwards, stopped for some reason opposite the Foxhall Hotel near the junction with Princess Street. The conductor has taken the opportunity to collect fares the easy way.

and in February 1914 ordered six more racks, to make 24 in all. This time they had found another source of second-hand equipment. In December 1913 they bought 25 GE52 motors from Sheffield Corporation who were replacing their old single-deck cars. Twelve of these motors went into the six 1914 toastracks. They were less powerful (at 25 h.p.) than the GE54s and were apparently lower-geared to suit Sheffield's hills.

The six cars arrived between June and July 1914, just weeks before the outbreak of the First World War. They were charged in the books at £510 each, presumably including the motors, which cost £47 per car.

Toastrack Operations

The Circular Tour was always run from Marton Depot, and the main batch of toastracks was traditionally housed there. The shed closed completely in the winter, apart from the annual Lost Property sale, when the toastracks provided the seating and the depot took on an almost ecclesiastical atmosphere, with row after row of varnished wooden pews.

The toastracks usually emerged from Marton at Easter. For a few years before the First World War, they had run right through from Easter to the end of the season, but thereafter they went back into hibernation between Easter and Whit. Nevertheless they accumulated

No. 70 seems to have mislaid its new headlamp in this view at Pleasure Beach in 1921, with Dreadnoughts 25 and 17 behind near Victoria Pier.

Car 70 in August 1926, taking the cast of "Brighter Blackpool" from the Winter Gardens to the Pleasure Beach. This is a still from "Happy Days in Blackpool" made by Parkstone Films of Lytham. One of the portly gentlemen organising the bright young things is John Jenkinson, a director of Parkstone. Many years later Peter Worden, the film historian, discovered the film in a shed at the Jenkinson's house at Wrea Green. This is one of the few frames not seriously affected by damp. *(PW)*

substantial mileages for open cars, averaging about 10,000 miles a year during the 1920s.

Although the racks are indelibly identified with the Circular Tour, only about 15% of their mileage was accounted for by the glamour route, and most of their time was spent trundling mundanely up and down the Promenade.

The racks were also regularly used as lunchtime and teatime extras on the town routes – two cars to Layton, two to

Palatine Road on the Marton route, and two more along Central Drive to Middle Lane (now St. Annes Road). When this happened, the toastracks' route boards were fixed in the horizontal position.

Other Duties

On Saturdays the toastracks were used as football specials on the Central Drive route. Blackpool F.C. were only in the Second Division at the time, but their matches attracted crowds of up to 20,000

when the football season overlapped the holiday season.

Before the match the toastracks shuttled between Central Station and Bloomfield Road, and then waited during the match on the Pleasure Beach sidings. But it was after the match that they really came into their own. The drivers didn't even stop their cars to load; they simply cruised slowly along on the first notch of power, while the crowd jumped on. The poor guard, clinging onto the side, had to collect as many fares as he could on the short trip into town.

The racks were also in their element on private sightseeing tours, which were just about the only occasions when Blackpool exercised its right to run over the Lytham tramways. In September 1917 a distinguished gathering of British tramway managers, in Blackpool for their annual conference, went to St. Annes by toastrack. And in August 1920 a party of children from war-damaged parts of France travelled in a decorated toastrack as far as Fairhaven.

When the Illuminations restarted in 1925, the toastracks were ideal for viewing the Lights if the weather was good. Normally they ran as Promenade extras, but for the first night of the 1930 Illuminations, 20 September, they were given a special service of their own. That evening, all thirty cars ran between Clifton Drive and Bispham. It was perhaps the toastracks' finest hour.

Cars 161 – 166 (1927)

The fleet of 24 Preston-built toastracks (Nos. 69 - 92) saw the Corporation comfortably through the First World

When the toastracks were not running on the Circular Tour or the Promenade, their route boards were fixed horizontally, as demonstrated by car 78 on its way home to Marton Depot in the evening sunshine during the early Twenties.

A formidable load for six Blackpool toastracks as the Women's Liberal Federation (plus one lone male) prepare to embark for a tour of Blackpool and St. Annes in May 1926. The photograph was only possible because the tracks between Church Street and Queens Square had been closed since 12 April for relaying. In the distance, car 29 is running on a special shuttle service to the Cabin, which was operated by five cars from Marton Depot. To reach North Promenade from Marton they reversed in Talbot Square and ran via Talbot Road and Dickson Road to the Gynn.

War and into the early 1920s. During this period the Tramways Department established a new tramcar maintenance works at Rigby Road which was so comprehensive that it was capable of producing complete trams from scratch. Between 1923 and 1929, 35 double–deck Standard cars were built there.

In November 1925 it was decided that the new works should also build six toastracks which, somebody believed, would be needed when the Circular Tour was eventually extended southwards to Squires Gate. This was a very odd decision, as Circular Tour revenue had fallen by half since the war. The decision looked odder still when the new Tour still hadn't materialised six years later.

Nevertheless the new racks were built, and allocated numbers 161 - 166, following on from the final batch of double-deckers. Being constructed on the

same underframes as the Standard cars, they were shorter than the pre-war racks and had one bench less, seating 64 instead of 69. Otherwise they looked identical, even to replicating the fancy seat-frames and tracery on the destination boxes.

Red to Green

When Walter Luff took over from Charles Furness as Blackpool's Transport Manager in January 1933, the first priority in his Five Year Plan was to replace much of the old tram fleet.

However all that happened to the toastracks at first was that their livery changed from red and white to green and cream. Some other older cars were simply given a quick coat of green paint over the red, and this may well have happened to the toastracks. Whether their steps and trolley mast did actually change from white to cream isn't clear:

there are no known colour views and the (rare) monochrome photographs of the toastracks in their green period don't help much. Nobody seems to remember whether the destination boards were repainted green.

Souped-up Toastracks

Although Luff had initially been rather dismissive about the toastracks, he seems to have grown rather fond of them. By 1934 he had already made modest improvements to some of them, even though their mileage reduced dramatically when the streamlined Boats arrived later that year.

Early in December 1933, No. 89, one of the racks with 25 h.p. motors from Sheffield, was fitted with the bogies (and 35 h.p. motors) from Fleetwood Box car 105 which had just been displaced by the new streamlined railcoaches. A toastrack with 70 h.p. was as powerful as a double-

No. 160 - The Unknown Toastrack

At first glance, just one more of the thousands of photographs taken at the Oxford Hotel – but toastrack number 160?

Blackpool Corporation built six toastracks in 1927, numbered 161 – 166, following on from Standard cars 142 – 160.

It was only during the preparation of this chapter that the long-accepted version of events began to look slightly suspect. There was very little official evidence, and much of it was circumstantial, but the facts didn't quite fit properly.

Basically two sets of dates are known for each tram – the day it was recorded as a "New Car" (presumably when it was completed and/or entered service) and the day it was first involved in an accident - or, more accurately, incident. Putting these two sets of dates together produced the following table:

Car	"New Car"	First Accident
156	12 May 1927	1 Aug. 1927
157	2 June 1927	10 Aug. 1927
158	8 June 1927	19 Aug. 1927
159	9 June 1927	30 July 1927
160	9 Sept. 1927	10 June 1927
161	12 July 1927	22 July 1927
162	14 July 1927	2 Aug. 1927
163	15 July 1927	9 Oct. 1927
164	19 July 1927	25 July 1927
165	No date	4 Aug. 1927
166	No date	6 Aug. 1928

Which raised several questions:

1. Why were there no "New Car" dates for toastracks 165 and 166?

2. How could Standard 160's first accident occur three months before the car was built?

3. How did toastrack 166 run till August 1928 without an accident?

Just before this book went to press, the conundrum was solved with the finding of the picture shown above. It was a most unlikely discovery. First of all, only a handful of photographs are known to exist of the 1927 toastracks in service. Secondly very few pictures taken at the Oxford Hotel show the number of the toastrack. And thirdly the Tramways Committee put a stop to the Oxford photographs on 25 July 1927. All the laws of probability were against it, but there it was – a toastrack bearing the number "160".

So what does it mean? Well, it doesn't explain why toastrack 165 has no "New Car" date, but it does clear up the other issues. It now looks certain that toastrack 166 was built in May or June 1927 as No. 160. In September 1927, when Standard car 160 was

completed, the toastrack was renumbered – the first Blackpool tram ever to change its number.

It also means that the toastrack now preserved as No. 166 at the National Tramway Museum has lost its claim to be the last new toastrack built anywhere in the world.

Standard car 160 soon after being built at Rigby Road in September 1927. Driver Jack Hartley is wearing the tram-driver's winter outfit of felt drayman's gloves and waterproof cape.

deck Standard car, but six tons lighter, so the difference in performance was quite significant. In fact it was on a par with the new Boats, which had 80 h.p. but rather more bodywork to carry round.

Pleased with the results, Luff upgraded seven more cars (80, 82, 86, 87, 88, 91 and 92) using motors from his previous employers the West Riding Tramways, who were scrapping their trams. These 70 h.p. cars became the flagships of the toastrack fleet – No. 82 ran over 3,000 miles in 1936 – whilst the twelve oldest cars (69 – 79 and 81, all dating from 1911/12) were very much the poor relations, not turning a wheel until August. The six newest cars (161 – 166) fared little better, No. 163 being the only one to reach 1,000 miles in 1936.

Toastracks Promoted

At the beginning of January 1936, No. 92, one of the 70 h.p. cars, went into the Body Shop for experimental surgery. Each row of seats was cut in the middle to produce a central gangway for the conductor, reducing the seating from 69 to 56.

Without waiting to see how No. 92 performed in service, the Transport Committee approved (as they usually did) Luff's proposal to rebuild all the toastracks in the same way. The sixth rebuild, No. 82, emerged during April 1936 in a striking new livery with a green "V" on a cream dash, and looking

Above: **Spot the toastrack. One of the problems in illustrating this book has been the self-effacing nature of the vehicle, and its tendency to disappear in a crowd. No. 165 is in there somewhere, accompanied by Standard car 143, Dreadnought 23 and Lytham No. 4 at the Tower some time around 1929. Something is going on, but it's not clear what; the police are out in force, but don't appear to be having much influence on events.** *(SD)*

Below: **The attractive green-V livery was sadly short-lived, at least in passenger service. This is No. 72 at the start of its last full season, reversing at Bispham on Easter Sunday, 9 April 1939. The driver is raising the off-side safety rails. The three-track layout was installed in 1934, ostensibly for turning cars during the Illuminations, but soon proved to be invaluable at all times of the season.** *(H.B. Priestley, National Tramway Museum)*

During 1941 the last surviving toastracks were lined up in the gloom of Rigby Road depot, its roof-lights painted over for the black-out. *(Richard Elliott/IM)*

as much like a Boat as a toastrack could. The "Circular Tour" route-boards survived, though now repainted in a stylish shaded lettering.

Upgrading the toastrack fleet restored the fortunes of some of the less favoured cars. The 70 h.p. racks were still the most frequently used, but the load was much more evenly spread across the whole class. The six smaller cars from 1927 started clocking up over 2,000 miles a year.

Destroyed by the RAF

The outbreak of war had been a foregone conclusion throughout 1939. But even with "war clouds hanging low", as the Traffic Diary recorded on 31 August 1939, the future still looked promising for Luff's burgeoning tourist

fleet. There were now 42 open trams and 24 open buses, all in the same magnificent streamlined livery and all new or refurbished within the past few years. Like the rest of the tram fleet, the toastracks were fitted with masks over their headlamps to reduce glare in the unlikely event of their being used after dark.

Perversely it wasn't the Luftwaffe who destroyed the Blackpool toastracks, but the Royal Air Force. The first blow came on 3 November 1939 when Marton Depot closed and was taken over by the Air Ministry as a training centre.

Despite this setback there was a deceptive air of normality about the Blackpool tramway during the first months of 1940, but once the Germans over-ran Northern Europe in May, the

pattern of tramway operations began to change drastically. Instead of crowds of visitors, the town was full of troops being trained, war workers being carried to the aircraft factory at Squires Gate, and evacuated civil servants being ferried to and from the requisitioned hotels where they now worked.

Overall the tramway system was busier than it had ever been, but the increase was very unevenly spread. Wartime traffic on the Squires Gate and Marton routes soared to two-and-a-half times its pre-war level, but the Promenade fell by 16%. More significantly for the toastracks, the seasonal peak virtually disappeared. In 1938 the daily turn-out of trams had ranged from 49 in January to 207 on August Bank Holiday. In a typical wartime year, 91 cars ran in January and only 113 in August.

This colossal change of emphasis hardly boded well for trams that could only be used in fine weather, on a system which had far too many cars and too little room to keep them. The effect had already been felt in 1940, when the toastracks made their last appearance as early as 9 August, which would normally have been their busiest period. Nine cars ran that day from Rigby Road.

Unfortunately Rigby Road was also on the RAF's list, and in July 1940 some of the works buildings there were requisitioned. Many of the redundant toastracks were moved to open storage in the yard of the old Tramroad Company depot at Copse Road, Fleetwood. As far as is known, it was the first trip that any of these cars had made north of Cleveleys.

It also turned out to be the last. In August 1940 toastracks 69 and 70, which thirty years earlier had started the phenomenal success of the Circular Tour, were scrapped. In July 1941 Luff was given approval to break up the remainder.

By the summer of 1942, only cars 80, 84, 86 and 91 of the original toastracks remained, plus five of the Blackpool-built cars, 162 - 166. Their licences had not been renewed on 1 April 1942, so they were unlikely to run again. Yet astonishingly the toastracks seem to have had one last day out. Traffic records show that eight racks were sent out on 12 July.

Once the summer was over, the four remaining large cars were broken up, No. 84 being the last to go in December 1942. The six smaller racks survived, but never ran in passenger service again. They were only 15 years old and hardly run in, with less than 50,000 miles on the clock, and one careful owner. For some, the best was yet to come.

Toastrack 83 awaits its end in the yard at Copse Road, where it was broken up in September 1941. Fleetwood Rack 126 survived as a works car until 1951. *(EF)*

Llandudno's four cars were the only toastracks still running in Britain after the Second World War. No. 22 is ready to leave Colwyn Bay on 2 July 1950 with another load of holiday-makers, some more enthusiastic than others. *(John H. Meredith)*

*T*he *Oxford English Dictionary's* definition of a toastrack is suitably crisp: "a contrivance for holding dry toast, keeping each piece on edge and separate; also a vehicle, especially a tram having full-width seats and (usually) open sides". The *OED* cites 1801 for the word's first vehicular use in Germany ("ein Tohstgestell") and 1905 for its first in English, but it was certainly in common usage before then. In 1898 the *Blackpool Herald* described the Fleetwood Tramroad's winter saloons as "a big improvement on the toastrack cars", and presumably its readers knew what it was talking about.

Nowadays (and, for clarity, in this book) the term "toastrack" is used for completely open vehicles, and "crossbench" for cars with a roof, although the roofed Fleetwood Tramroad cars continue to be known as Fleetwood Racks, which doesn't help much.

The electric toastrack tram was a peculiarly British phenomenon. As far as is known - it's impossible to be absolutely sure - the genuine electric toastrack existed nowhere else in the world. This was odd because horse-drawn toastracks were once quite common, being cheaper to build, easier to pull and quicker to load than enclosed trams. And since there were no motors to fit under the floor, horse-drawn toastracks were lower and easier to board than their electric counterparts.

Crossbench Cars

In the electric era, however, the roofed crossbench car rapidly became the standard open vehicle in the USA, perhaps because electric trams needed support for the trolley. Crossbench cars were amazingly popular in America; there were 3,500 in the state of Massachusetts alone.

Britain had nothing on that scale. But since the first electric tramways tended to

British Electric Toastrack Trams

Built	Cars	No.	Builder	Wheels	Withdrawn
1911	Blackpool 69–70	2	Preston	8	1940
1912	Blackpool 71–76	6	Preston	8	1941
1912	Blackpool 77–80	4	Preston	8	1941–42
1913	Blackpool 81–86	6	Preston	8	1941–42
1914	Southport 21	1	Preston	4	1930–32
1914	Blackpool 87–92	6	Preston	8	1941–42
1914	Southport 23–27	3	Preston	4	1930–32
1916	Southampton 2	1	[Preston]	4	1936
1919	Rothesay 11–12	2	Rothesay	8	1936
1919	Southport 29–33	3	Preston	4	1930–32
1920	Llandudno 19–22	4	Preston	8	1955
1921	Rothesay 22	1	Rothesay	4	1936
1927	Blackpool 161–166	6	Blackpool	8	1942

The shores of the Pacific might be 5,000 miles away, but Cornwall's only tramway, serving the tin-mining towns of Camborne and Redruth, bought two of these stylish little "California" four-wheelers from Milnes in 1902. *(EF)*

follow American practice and import American equipment, the crossbench car gained a tenuous foothold over here. Several early systems - not all of them holiday resorts - bought crossbench cars. But the climate was much less suitable than in America, and the crossbench car had fallen from favour by the turn of the century. Altogether only 34 double-deck and 99 single-deck crossbench cars ran in Britain, most of them on the Fylde Coast or the Isle of Man.

Combination Cars

Although seaside tramways still bought the occasional new crossbench car, most other tramways with a taste for the open air turned instead to combination cars, sometimes known as "California cars" from the state where the idea originated. These combined one or two open sections with one or two short saloons, and seemed to offer the best of both worlds. In practice the passengers usually all wanted to be outside or all inside.

Combination cars were surprisingly popular with operators, if not passengers, and nearly 400 were built for 28 different British tramways in some fairly un-Californian locations. Operators in Lancashire and the North-East seemed to have a particularly rosy view of their

climate, the largest users being Manchester (with 62), followed by such exotic places as Newcastle, Wigan, Rochdale, Middleton, Cardiff, Darlington, Gateshead, Rothesay and Southport, in that order. The last two were the only seaside resorts in the list.

The combination car in turn went out of fashion when the open toastrack began its brief heyday just before and after the First World War.

Mount Lowe

Whilst the Giant's Causeway tramway *(page 89)* could legitimately claim to have operated the first open electric car in the world in 1883, it wasn't a toastrack. The first electric toastrack could very nearly be credited to the spectacular 3 ft. 6 ins. gauge tramway on Mount Lowe near Los Angeles, which started operations in 1894 with two four-wheel electric cars. They were standard American cross-bench cars without the roof - at 4,000 feet the climate on the mountain was more amenable to such cars than it was at sea-level in California.

The main body of the two Mount Lowe cars was pure toastrack, but the arrangements for the trolley were slightly compromised, consisting of a long gantry down the centre of the tram. Over the years this grew, first into a folding canopy and eventually into a full roof, which ultimately disqualified the Mount Lowe cars from the exclusive Toastrack Club.

Canada's Electric Charabancs

Whilst discussing transatlantic precursors of the true toastrack, another honourable mention should be given to a magnificent vehicle developed in 1905 by the Montreal Street Railway - the tiered observation car.

This design was so successful that eventually most of the major Canadian cities had similar cars. They were really an electric version of the old charabanc - completely open, with crossbench seats rising towards the rear - but decorated with fancy wrought-iron work, and looking rather like the dress circle of the Grand Theatre coming down the street. Calgary's version was even panelled with plate glass mirrors.

These tiered observation cars were unique to Canada, where they were remarkably long-lived; some were still running as late as 1958. It's a pity Blackpool never borrowed the idea; they would have looked magnificent on the Circular Tour.

The British Toastrack Family

But Blackpool had set the standard for the British toastrack in 1911, and thereafter they stuck to it. Indeed there

Canada's spectacular tiered observation cars lasted a remarkably long time. Car 3 is taking part in the closing ceremony of the Montreal tramways on 30 August 1959. *(VL)*

The Anatomy of the Toastrack

Dash panel   Controller   Controller key   Brake   Ratchet

*I*n vehicular terms the toastrack tram was the ultimate triumph of function over form – the elemental public transport vehicle, consisting of a platform full of seats, mounted on wheels, with something to make it go and something to make it stop.

The driving position of a toastrack reflected this basic simplicity. It's difficult to imagine any powered vehicle having fewer controls – no gears, no steering wheel, no pedals in the normal sense, other than one to sound the gong and another to drop sand on the rails if they were wet.

To start the tram, the driver simply set the controller key to forward or reverse, and turned the controller handle. To stop it, he turned the brake handle. To keep it stopped, he kicked the ratchet in. To immobilise it, he removed the controller key.

Above: **A distinctive feature of the Llandudno toastracks was the sloping floor. Regular working on a toastrack was liable to leave a tram driver with one leg longer than the other.** *(Eric Thornton/GP)*

Below: **The archetypal toastrack – a Blackpool car at the Oxford Hotel. On the trolley mast is the usual Blackpool warning notice to passengers. The lights in the ends of the destination box have been removed, which dates the picture to the period after 1921, when proper head and tail lights were fitted in the dash panels.**

Guard rail   Dog gate   Running board   Bogie   Brake block   Axle box   Sand pipe   Lifeguard tray

was a strong family resemblance to all the 45 toastracks that ever ran in Britain. This was partly because most were built at Preston, but also because the toastrack, being such a primitive vehicle, didn't lend itself to variations on the theme.

Nevertheless within its overall simplicity, the toastrack posed several inherent design problems, which operators approached in different ways.

Four Wheels Good …

The most obvious issue facing the prospective toastrack buyer was the choice of four or eight wheels. Four-wheel cars were cheaper and could negotiate tighter curves. Southport and Southampton, like the majority of British systems, never used anything but four-wheelers.

The other three toastrack users were primarily bogie-car systems, though they all had at least one four-wheeler. Blackpool had a short and salutary experience of modern four-wheel trucks under De Luxe cars 62 - 64 in 1911, and never bought another. Llandudno and Rothesay also favoured bogies for their toastracks, though Rothesay later built a four-wheeler – the only one on the line.

Bogie cars rode much more smoothly than four-wheelers, especially toastracks, where the absence of the usual dropped platforms allowed the bogies to be placed further apart than usual.

Lifeguards

The drawback of having the bogies nearer the ends of the car was that it reduced the space for the lifeguard mechanism. This normally had two parts

Above: Southport's seven cars were much the largest fleet of four-wheeled toastracks in Britain. No. 27, the last of the 1914 batch, was photographed at Duke Street in 1915. The steps on the offside are folded up to reduce clearance problems in Southport's narrow streets. The lettering on the fender reads "45 Minutes' Drive Round the Town" in blue on a white background.

Left: The curious arrangement of lifeguard originally fitted to Llandudno's toastracks.

Below: For a short period, Blackpool's first two toastracks, Nos. 69 and 70, ran with lifeguard trays but no gates. No. 69 is posing at Devonshire Square in August 1911. *(BL)*

- a gate at the front, which activated a tray just ahead of the bogies to catch anybody who fell under the tram.

As delivered, the first two Blackpool cars had the tray, but no room for the gate. Soon afterwards a rather gimcrack gate was fixed, suspended from a bar which projected about a foot beyond the fender and looked as likely to cause injuries as prevent them. Gimcrack or not, this became the standard arrangement at Blackpool.

The two other systems with bogie cars had different solutions. Rothesay's toastracks were so long that there was still room for a full gate and tray in front of the bogies, but Llandudno got into an even worse mess than Blackpool. As built, they had a similar arrangement to Blackpool's, but with a gate which projected so far that it had a net attached to stop people falling behind it – a sort of lifeguard for the lifeguard. Apparently each car only carried one net, which had to be moved from end to end. Later photographs show a gate more like Blackpool's, but by 1930 the entire contraption had been replaced by a simple four-bar metal plough guard.

Steps

One of the toastrack's greatest advantages was its speed of loading. Charles Furness reckoned that Blackpool could reload a toastrack in 90 seconds; as the old passengers got off at one side, the new ones got on at the other.

It may have seemed efficient to the management, but for the individual passenger the getting-on was rarely easy and the getting-off harder still. The *Blackpool Gazette* wrote in 1934 that "to get aboard the toastracks with their high awkward steps and narrow seats, has been an ordeal to everybody, and to elderly ladies has been a positive nightmare. There have been innumerable instances of these folk getting wedged fast and having to be dragged out by force."

Bogie cars were particularly awkward, because they had to be higher off the ground than a four-wheeler, to leave room for the bogies to swing out on curves. To make things worse, the steps couldn't run for the whole length of the car. The three bogie systems each tackled this problem in different ways.

Blackpool borrowed a rather crude arrangement from the Fleetwood Tramroad, whereby the step was raised about nine inches above each wheel, then down between the two axles, and then up again. This "paddlebox" layout made the cars uncomfortably wide, and meant that at places on the Marton route toastracks couldn't pass each other.

Llandudno, which had clearance

Those were the days, when traffic on the A55 trunk road along the North Wales coast would come to a halt while the conductor got off to help a local passenger gamely boarding Llandudno No. 21 in Colwyn Bay. The coaches may have had quite a wait, since the second step was, if anything, worse than the first.

problems in Colwyn Bay, used folding steps. They were neater and narrower than Blackpool's, but even more awkward for passengers, particularly over the bogies, where there was a tiny folding step, about a foot long.

The Rothesay cars, which had maximum-traction bogies with one wheel smaller than the other, were lower than the Blackpool cars, but still only the most athletic passengers chose the seats over the bogies.

Handles

To mount the steps, passengers were provided with handles on the ends of each seat. UEC had a neat style of double handle, which was standard on all the Preston-built toastracks, including the Southampton car.

The grab handles were attached to cast iron seat frames. These were perforated, presumably to save weight, with a pattern which was one of the few decorative elements on the entire tram. Again UEC had a standard design which they had used on several overseas orders, and this now appeared at Blackpool, Southport, Southampton and Llandudno.

The most stylish metalwork was on Rothesay's home-built toastracks, which had elegant curvaceous seat frames, looking rather as though Charles Rennie Mackintosh had designed them, and neatly doubling as handles.

Seats

Once passengers had hauled themselves aboard, they would find very similar seating arrangements on all the toastracks

The extreme length of Rothesay's bogie cars allowed room for a proper lifeguard mechanism, and the use of maximum-traction bogies reduced the problems of the steps. Rothesay had an elegant design of seat frame which served as grab-handles, and instead of the usual Preston safety rail, used chains between the seats.

Strand Road Car Works - The Toastrack Builders

Of the 45 toastracks which ever ran in Britain, 35 were built at Preston, six were virtual replicas of the same design, and one was assembled from parts made there. So the car works at Preston clearly played a significant rôle in the story of the British toastrack.

Strand Road's First Tram

The works was built during 1864 on the Strand, an area of marshland next to the River Ribble, by the North of England Railway Carriage & Iron Company. Railway wagons were the staple product, but the first vehicle produced at the works was one of the earliest open tramcars in Britain, built for a remarkable tramway on Southport Pier.

The pier, then the longest in the country, was opened in August 1860. It was so long that in May 1863 a narrow-gauge tramway was introduced down the middle of the pier to take passengers to the steamers which ran across the Ribble to Blackpool. The rolling-stock consisted of a tiny open four-wheeled carriage, about ten feet long, carrying ten passengers, and the motive power comprised as many able-bodied men as the load required to push it against the prevailing wind.

During the winter of 1864/65 this primitive tramway was replaced by a much more sophisticated and substantial 3 ft. 6 ins. gauge line running down the south side of the pier. It was operated by a very early version of cable traction - eight years before San Francisco introduced cable cars - powered from an engine house in the middle of the pier.

To inaugurate the new line, the carriage works at Preston built a larger vehicle, roughly twice the size of the original (which became a trailer). Completed in February 1865, it was twenty feet long, and seated around 24 passengers on long knifeboard seats.

This sideways-on toastrack was, as far as is known, the only tram ever built by the Preston Wagon Company, as they were commonly known. Unfortunately the Company didn't build too many wagons either, and only once managed to pay a dividend on their substantial capital of £124,000.

As the trade depression of the late 1870s deepened, the shareholders decided to cut their losses – by then the shares were practically worthless – and the works closed in November 1878. The building and contents were sold for £25,000 in October 1879. The stock of materials was removed, but the machinery was left in place, pending a revival in trade.

The ER&TCW

With the depression dragging on through the 1880s, the revival didn't come for twenty years. Early in 1898 the works was bought by a group led by the directors of the Fleetwood Tramroad, who had seen an opportunity to satisfy the growing demand for electric trams by adopting American techniques of mass production.

They extended the old car works, equipped it with the latest American machinery, and re-opened it as the Electric Railway & Tramway Carriage Works in March 1899. In the following year a sister factory, the English Electric Manufacturing Company, opened on the west side of Strand Road, to produce electrical equipment.

Although the ER&TCW was too

The very first vehicle completed at Strand Road – and the first of over 8,000 trams – was this unusual sideways-on toastrack for the Southport Pier tramway in 1865. The line was a genuine cable tramway, where the car could grip or release the cable. Passengers sat on a centre "knifeboard" seat; if they all sat on one side, the car tended to derail. The passengers are H.R.H. Princess May and her husband the Duke of Teck, setting off down the pier on what is thought to have been the first royal tram ride in Britain, on 9 October 1872. *(The Graphic)*

This is where most of Britain's toastracks were built – the Electric Railway & Tramway Carriage Works' new Body Shop at Strand Road, Preston. In this early view, single-deckers are being built for Dudley and the Potteries. The other cars are for customers with close connections to Strand Road: the double-decker is for the Carlisle tramways, with which the founders of the ER&TCW and the Fleetwood Tramroad were closely involved. On the right is a horse car for the North Metropolitan Tramways, whose chairman George Richardson was also chairman of the ER&TCW and the Tramroad Company. *(Arthur Winter)*

late to enjoy the short-lived boom in British crossbench cars during the 1890s, the Preston works made quite a speciality of crossbench and combination cars for overseas customers. Some of the fittings used in these cars appeared later in the toastracks which Preston built for British systems.

The ER&TCW was a very successful operation, and in 1904 absorbed several of its competitors, renaming itself the United Electric Car Company. In 1919, in another merger, it became English Electric.

Between 1899 and 1936 the car works at Preston built nearly 5,000 trams for

Britain and 3,800 for export. Orders dried up in the 1930s – apart from the Blackpool streamliners – and in 1937 the plant switched to aircraft manufacture, which lasted until the works closed in September 1993. All the buildings on the east of Strand Road were demolished in 1994. The West works remained open.

To the left of the Body Shop in the picture above was the original 1864 carriage works where the Southport Pier car had been built. The ER&TCW didn't build many trams in the old shop, but here it is being used for Liverpool cars 54 – 87, which can be seen in almost every stage of construction. Both photographs were taken in the spring of 1900, and are reproduced by courtesy of the Harris Museum and Art Gallery. *(Arthur Winter)*

- long wooden benches with reversible backs, seating five passengers on standard gauge cars and four on the narrow gauge (except for Rothesay who managed five).

The number of benches varied remarkably, being different for each of the six varieties of toastrack. Rothesay's bogie cars had sixteen rows, followed by Llandudno with fifteen. Blackpool had fourteen, and thirteen on its home-built cars. Of the four-wheelers the Southport/Southampton cars had ten benches and Rothesay nine.

The main problem with the seating was what to do about the trolley mast. Blackpool's solution was to divide the middle row into smaller two-seat benches with a gap for the trolley. Southport took a different approach, and fixed two seats back-to-back fore and aft of the mast, so that one row of passengers was always travelling backwards. This arrangement didn't leave much headroom for the two passengers in the middle with their backs to the trolley, and wouldn't have worked for the Blackpool cars in 1911, when women's hats reached enormous proportions. But by 1914, when the Southport cars were built, fashions had become more restrained.

Rothesay and Llandudno copied Blackpool, but Llandudno added a new variation by fixing the last two benches back-to-back, giving passengers on the rear seat a panoramic view of the tramway's splendid scenery.

Wartime conductresses everywhere were unhappy with the gymnastics required to collect fares on a toastrack. In March 1917 Southampton, with a touch of Southern chivalry, divided its bench seats down the middle to "enable the girls to remain on the car away from any risk of accident". The capacity fell from 50 to 40, which was no doubt why conductresses at Blackpool, Southport and Rothesay had to make the best of things. It was twenty years before Blackpool followed Southampton's example, and the other two never did.

To prevent passengers rather than conductresses falling off, the Board of Trade required toastracks to have a wooden bar at elbow height on the off-side of the tram. This was again a standard Preston fitment, usually divided into three sections, and hinged so that it swung down neatly against the underframe when the car was reversed. Rothesay used chains instead.

Destination Displays

There was nowhere on the end of a toastrack to mount the usual destination box. Llandudno, with only one route, got round this by having a slot on the dash to hold a discreet metal plate with "Llandudno" on one side and "Colwyn Bay" on the other. There were plates for other short-workings and one for "Special Car" which appears on a multitude of photographs taken on enthusiasts' tours.

Blackpool went to the other extreme and emblazoned the words "Circular Tour" and "Promenade" on each side of a huge reversible wooden board above the driver's head. Southport copied Blackpool, except that they had "Grand Tour" instead of "Promenade".

The boards at Blackpool and Southport were painted in fleet livery, with red lettering on white at Blackpool, and red on cream at Southport. There is a suspicion that in the early days at Blackpool, the "Promenade" lettering may have been black since it appears distinctly darker than the "Circular Tour" side of the board.

Both Blackpool and Southport hung supplementary boards from the main board, usually showing the fares. Blackpool placed theirs at one side, but Southport's was in the middle, where it must have obscured the vision of any driver above average height. On the back of their small boards Southport, whose tracks were closer together than Blackpool's, had the message "Passengers are warned not to let their arms project over the sides of the car".

Rothesay - ever different - had a neater four-sided board (rather reminiscent of destination indicators at the turn of the century) showing three destinations and "Depot". Southampton's toastrack, with no set route, didn't have boards, and like the Llandudno cars, always looked slightly naked at the ends.

Instead of boards, Southampton relied solely on a double-sided destination box, fitted with orthodox linen blinds, on the trolley mast. The other two larger systems, Blackpool and Southport had similar destination boxes. These were supported by scrollwork brackets as a small token to traditional tramcar design. Blackpool religiously copied these fancy brackets when they built Britain's last new toastracks in 1927. The workshops at Crich had to repeat the process when they restored No. 166.

Liveries

Toastracks were deeply frustrating for a generation of coach-painters accustomed to the painstaking application of traditional liveries in multiple coats of two or more colours with elaborate lining and fancy corner-pieces. On toastracks they quickly ran out of things to paint, and two-tone liveries were usually reduced to a single colour on the dash and the seat frames.

Another problem for the coach-painters was finding somewhere to put the undertaking's title. Generally municipal tramways were keener on this than companies, who preferred to fill any vacant space with advertisements. On toastracks there was little room for either.

In the early thirties it became fashionable to change liveries. Red went out of favour, partly because it was often used by competing bus companies. Blackpool changed to green, and Rothesay to blue.

But the only really imaginative livery applied to any of the toastracks was the spectacular cream-and-green-V colour scheme which the Blackpool cars carried all too briefly in the late Thirties. Who knows, perhaps No. 166, now preserved at the National Tramway Museum, will wear it again one day.

Southport Corporation made the most of the limited display space on a toastrack. By this late stage - July 1932 - the "45 Minutes' Drive" sign had been moved up from the fender to the bottom of the dash, still with its impeccable punctuation. *(EO)*

Much as Blackpool's open trams were admired and enjoyed over the years, nobody would claim that they had a dramatic impact on the rest of the British tramway industry. But they did have a profound effect on Blackpool's own bus fleet, which over the years included a variety of unusual open single-deckers - rubber-tyred versions of, first, the toastracks and then the Boats.

The Runabout Bus

Before the First World War, motor charabancs - larger versions of those which the Fleetwood Tramroad once used on the Pilling Tour - had superseded horse-drawn vehicles for pleasure trips. But it was only after the development of heavy-duty motor vehicles for wartime use that the bus became a serious rival to the tram in the cut-and-thrust of urban running.

One of the first steps in this process came about in the early Twenties when several seaside resorts - usually those which didn't have trams on their seafront - introduced "runabout" buses. The

Preparing one of the 1928 Leyland Lions for service at Rigby Road after it had been rebuilt with an open runabout body in August 1937. In the background, four toastracks share a nearly empty tram depot with two brand-new Brush cars and a double-deck Standard.

word originally meant a pedlar, but had been applied to light motor vehicles, and eventually became the accepted term for an open-sided bus.

Bournemouth introduced the first runabouts - three Guys - in 1923, and Southport bought one in December that year, but Blackpool didn't follow suit until 1926.

The Mysterious Motor Tour

Blackpool were quicker off the mark with a tourist bus route, introducing one as early as June 1922. It was the Corporation's first bus service in Blackpool, although they had been running an out-of-town route between Cleveleys and Thornton railway station since July 1921.

The Cleveleys route was operated by two small Tilling-Stevens petrol-electric buses, Nos. 1 and 2, but for much of the day the timetable only required a single bus. To occupy the spare vehicle, the

Tramways Department on 15 June 1922 introduced what they described as a "Special Motor Tour". It was a very low-key affair with no publicity, and there is no record of where the Tour went, how often it ran, or what the fare was. However it operated for the rest of the 1922 season, taking around £7 a week, with a maximum of £12.

In July 1922 the Corporation bought a third bus, which was much more suitable for touring - an open-top Tilling-Stevens double-decker seating 50 passengers. Common sense suggests that No. 3 was the mainstay of the Special Tour, though there's no direct evidence.

Buses to Stanley Park

The Corporation, with its huge fleet of toastrack trams, had little need for runabout buses until 1925, when they opened the New Park, which was officially named Stanley Park by Lord Derby in October 1926. The Park was

some way from the Marton tram route, and at first was poorly patronised. To overcome this the Corporation planned two bus services from the town centre.

The first was an extension to the Park Gates of an existing route from Adelaide Place (another Tramways Department pseudonym for the Tower); this became the No. 8 service when the bus routes were given numbers in June 1926. The second route was a circular from Talbot Square along the Drive which was being built right round the Park. Being a seasonal service, it didn't have a number at first, but eventually became Route 20.

The Freighters (35 – 38)

To operate the Park Circular the Corporation bought their first real "tourist" buses, and remarkable vehicles they were, looking suspiciously like the front half of a toastrack tram. There was no visible engine, and the driver had what appeared to be tramcar controls though, unlike tram drivers, he operated them sitting down.

The Corporation had been given a demonstration of a Shelvoke & Drewry

Above: **Tilling-Stevens bus No. 1 (left) and double-decker No. 3 operated Blackpool's first tourist bus service in June 1922. No. 6 didn't arrive until 1923.**

Below: **The first tourist bus on the Fylde Coast was this Guy runabout, which Lytham St. Annes Corporation put into service at Whitsuntide 1925 on the new Promenade between St. Annes and Fairhaven Lake. The runabout, seen here with its gaitered driver outside the Town Hall, eventually became No. 13 in the Lytham St. Annes fleet, and lasted until 1939, when it was transferred to Civil Defence work.**

The Fabulous Freighters

Freighter seems an odd name for a bus, but indicates its origin rather than its use. The Letchworth firm of Shelvoke & Drewry had developed the design in 1922 as a low-loading freight carrier, and had already built some 250 chassis for a variety of purposes, most conspicuously as dustcarts - Lytham St. Annes bought one early in 1926. Between 1922 and 1955, S&D built some 3,000 Freighters, most of them for municipal use.

The Freighter had a turning circle of only 21 ft. 8 ins. - less than a London taxi - and was steered not by a wheel but by a "tiller" on the right hand side of the driver. At his left hand the driver had another tiller to control the gears. In cold weather, experienced operators were known to drive with their hands in their pockets, working the tillers with their elbows. There were three forward and three reverse gears, and Freighters could be driven backwards just as fast as forwards if the driver stood up and used the tillers the wrong way round — not much use for a bus, but handy for a tipping wagon.

"Fast" was a relative term. Even in top gear the 13 h.p. engine of the Freighters could only manage 15 m.p.h. It was perhaps as well that this was not far removed from the 12 m.p.h. speed limit for buses, since the Freighter had no speedometer - or any other instruments for that matter. And 15 m.p.h. on a Freighter, with its tiny solid-tyred wheels, was probably quite fast enough for most passengers.

Above: **Freighter 38 at Stanley Park in 1926.**

Right: **No. 35 at Adelaide Place terminus, near the Tower, in 1926. Like all Blackpool's early buses, the Freighters were operated by one man. Their transmission system and tram-like controls made them ideal for tram drivers doing occasional extra turns on the buses.**

Below: **Freighter No. 38 was supposed to carry 24 passengers. Behind 38 is a Leyland Lioness. In the background a Tilling-Stevens is arriving on the Park service, with a Guy runabout heading up North Park Drive on the Park Circular.**

Freighter on 26 April 1926 and a week later ordered four, which became Nos. 35 to 38. As with the toastrack trams, Blackpool reduced the vehicle to its bare essentials, finishing up with the only open-top Freighter buses ever built.

They were also the only complete buses built by Shelvoke & Drewry, who normally supplied just the chassis and cab, for £455. Of course it didn't require great body-making skills to add steps and six rows of seats to a Freighter chassis, and the total cost only came to £573.

Blackpool wasn't the first seaside bus undertaking to spot the Freighter's potential. An operator at Worthing had bought Freighter chassis No. 10 in 1923, mounted an enclosed bus body on it, and labelled it the "Tram-o-car" (Worthing didn't have trams, so there was no confusion). It was so successful that Worthing eventually had fourteen Freighter buses, the second largest fleet of all after Crosville in North Wales who had fifteen. Altogether S&D built about 50 buses, the last in 1938; other users included Bournemouth and Plymouth, each with six.

The first two Blackpool vehicles entered service on Sunday 25 July 1926, right at the peak of the season. The roads round the Park weren't finished, so the Freighters were used as auxiliaries on the Adelaide Place route, where they provoked a rare moment of enthusiasm from the clerk who compiled the Traffic Department's records - normally laconic in the extreme. On 25 July he wrote: "Two freighters (runabouts) took up service 11.00 a.m. and 11.10 a.m. and proved a great attraction".

The "Monstre" Runabouts (45 - 50)

The Freighters remained on the Adelaide

Brand-new Guy runabout No. 47 during the inaugural weekend of the Stanley Park Circular on Easter Monday 1927. The passengers, collars turned up against the weather, hardly seem to be relishing this new experience and as usual the driver, wearing his tram "Motorman" badge, looks to be enjoying himself most.

One of the passengers sent this postcard to Liverpool with the message: "How's this? Notice I was not driving, tho' I observed the one who did so. Bang went sixpence on this tour. B'pool is pretty full, but the weather is real it." Which one sent it? The boy at the front was doubtless up-to-date with the latest Twenties slang, but wouldn't have paid 6d. - nor would his father. Hardly likely to be the lady on row two - or any of the other women for that matter. Probably the man on the third row.

Place route, leaving the Corporation short of buses for the forthcoming Park Circular. Popular though the Freighters undoubtedly were with the public, the Corporation were having second thoughts, and looking for something more flexible.

They settled on the Guy BB chassis and in November 1926 ordered three. In December they increased the order to four. Guy had made quite a speciality of small-wheeled runabouts; Lytham had bought a roofed crossbench Guy in June 1925 for its Promenade tourist route. But small wheels implied solid tyres, which were becoming less and less acceptable.

So the Blackpool Guys had pneumatic tyres and full-sized wheels. To keep the seats low, the chassis was sunk between the axles.

The Guys, unlike the Freighters, had windscreens, and were certainly impressive vehicles, albeit looking more like ladderless fire-engines than buses. The *Blackpool Times* described them, with archaic spelling, as "Monstre Runabouts". Although they dwarfed the tiny Freighters and cost half as much again at £925, they carried only six more passengers - 30 altogether on eight benches, one of which faced backwards where the rear axle intruded.

The Stanley Park Circular

The new runabouts entered service on Good Friday, 15 April 1927, launching the Park Circular Tour from Talbot Square – a five-mile journey for 6d. They were a huge success that Easter, taking 10,700 passengers on more than 400 trips and quite stealing the thunder from the tram Circular Tour, which only carried 7,700 passengers that weekend.

On the strength of these figures, the Corporation immediately ordered two more runabouts, which arrived in July and became Nos. 49 and 50. They looked similar to the first four and cost the same, but were shorter and wider, seating 32 passengers on seven benches.

Although the Park Circular couldn't hope to maintain its initial level of patronage, it became a regular seasonal attraction. Like the tram Circular, however, its popularity steadily declined in the late Twenties, and by 1933

For all their fearsome appearance, the Guy runabouts seated only six more than the tiny Freighters. No. 50, seen in Talbot Square, has the wider seating and shorter rear overhang of the last two Guys, with one less bench.

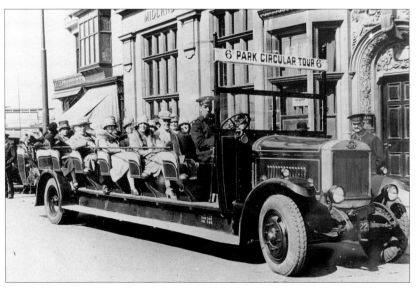

passenger figures had fallen from 115,000 to 16,000.

Freighters Withdrawn

The Freighters on the No. 8 route seemed particularly prone to rear-end collisions. Perhaps the braking system - a combination of foot-brake and transmission brake applied via the gear tiller - was too complicated or simply not powerful enough.

The first to be withdrawn was No. 36, which ran into the back of No. 37 on 6 August 1930. No. 37 in turn ended its career with a bang - probably rather louder and more destructive - when it collided with Standard car 41 on 10 September 1931.

Nos. 35 and 38 lasted until 1932. News of their impending withdrawal merited a mention in the *Evening Gazette* - a rare accolade for a bus: "The motor runabouts which have been so popular on the service to Stanley Park have become the worse for wear, and the Town Council has decided to replace them with four 26-seat saloon buses with sunshine roofs."

The withdrawal of the Freighters reduced the runabout fleet to just the six Guys, which soldiered on alone through the summers of 1933 and 1934.

The Gondolas (114 - 119)

When Walter Luff became Blackpool's

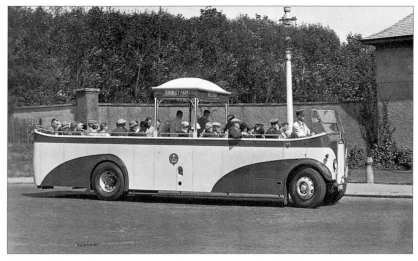

The Gondolas featured on a series of picture postcards of Blackpool's "super" new trams and buses. This is No. 117 at Stanley Park in July 1935.

Transport Manager in 1933, he concentrated on updating the tram fleet, and the few new buses he bought were fairly orthodox vehicles, apart from having centre entrances, which were just coming into vogue.

From 1935 onwards, however, Luff introduced virtually a complete new bus fleet, with the same streamlined styling as his new trams. Within two years there were bus equivalents of the open Boats, the single-deck railcoaches and the enclosed double-deckers.

The first to appear, for the 1935

season, were six magnificent open single-deckers, built on Leyland Lion four-cylinder petrol-engined chassis. By this time Blackpool normally used the more powerful six-cylinder Tiger chassis for its single-deckers, and indeed Burlingham built the bodies for twelve Tiger saloons (Nos. 102 - 113) alongside the new runabouts.

The first three buses were licensed on 28 June 1935, and the second three on 12 July. Just as the Freighters looked like half a toastrack, so the new buses closely resembled the Boats. They even had the

New Gondola 116 passes Central Station on its way back to the Promenade from Stanley Park on 5 August 1935. In the background Standard car 35 prepares to depart for South Pier. *(Leyland Journal/BCVM)*

Six new Leyland Lions, 59 - 64, show off their English Electric bodywork outside the workshops at Rigby Road in June 1928. These Lions, plus another six with different bodies, were converted to open runabouts in 1937. *(BCVM)*

same central arch, which served as the trolley tower on the trams, but was now turned into an elegant pagoda-like canopy, and gave the buses their nickname of Gondolas (or "Gond*o*las" as it was usually pronounced in Lancashire). The arch was slightly domed and hollow, the space inside being reserved for batteries in case the buses carried lights during the Illuminations.

There was accommodation for 35 passengers on stylish seats of teak and ash. In an article entitled "Combining Beauty with Utility in Seaside Rolling Stock" in the *Leyland Journal*, Luff explained that the seats were shaped so that, should it ever rain in Blackpool, the water would run off and drain away through concealed holes in the floor, which was slightly concave.

If necessary the buses could even be

covered. Luff said that "it would merely be necessary to remove the destination indicator in the central canopy and incorporate a covered roof, provision for the fastening of which exists at front and rear", which doesn't make it clear whether the conversion was meant to be long-term or just for a rainy day.

The Lions (55 - 66)

Alongside the elegant new Gondolas, the six 1927 Guy runabouts looked older than ever. To replace them, somebody had the inspired idea of putting Gondola-style bodies on the chassis of twelve redundant Leyland Lions, Nos. 55 - 66. These buses, new in 1928 with bodies by three different builders, had been the work-horses of the fleet, but were now little used after the influx of Luff's streamlined buses.

Although nearly as old as the Guys they were to replace, the Lions were still mechanically sound, and fitted in well with the prevailing plan for an all-Leyland fleet. In mid-1937 they were sent to Charles Roe's factory at Leeds for rebodying. Roe's quote for the job – £101 per bus – was far too good to miss. Indeed it was too good to be true, as Roe had forgotten to include the cost of the seats.

The new bodies were extremely stylish, being similar to the Gondolas but without the central canopy. The crews must have been pleased to find that the multiplicity of blinds on the Gondolas had been reduced on the Lions to two. As with the Gondolas, there was no route number.

The first rebuilds came back from Leeds at the end of July 1937. That year the Lions replaced four of the Guy runabouts, but Nos. 45 and 46 lasted for another season and made a brief appearance in August 1938.

The Cheetahs (19 - 24)

A fleet of eighteen runabouts really ought to have been enough, but something or somebody convinced Luff that he needed more. In September 1938 the Corporation, sunnily ignoring the gathering war clouds, ordered another six, along with six single-deck saloons and twelve double-deckers, plus twelve open-sided "sun saloon" trams to replace the venerable Fleetwood Racks.

The chassis chosen for the runabouts was the relatively new Leyland Cheetah, which was lighter than the Lion and Tiger, and ideal for an open bus. The

From ugly ducklings into swans. This is No. 61, the third vehicle in the line-up above and the first to be rebuilt, ready to leave the Roe factory at Leeds in July 1937.

Open-top Cheetah No. 19 at Central Station in May 1959. The Cheetahs spent much of their time on the 24 service, which was a modern version of the old Layton and Central Drive tram routes; many years earlier the toastrack trams had operated as summer relief vehicles on these routes. *(Robert Mack)*

Corporation normally used diesels by this time, but didn't like the idea of runabout passengers travelling round in a cloud of diesel smoke, and again opted for petrol engines, which were £150 cheaper. Perhaps they calculated that the extra fuel consumption wouldn't be significant on buses which only ran in summer.

Roe quoted £323 for the body (this time including the seats) but Burlinghams of Blackpool got the order at £330; the Corporation was always under pressure to support the local firm. In concept the bodies were similar to the Roe-bodied Lions, but the Corporation later altered the specification to add low glass windows, which gave the Cheetahs quite a different side aspect from the other runabouts. From the front they looked very similar to twelve single-deck saloons which Burlingham had built in 1937; in fact the destination display was identical, and at last included a route number blind.

By the time Burlingham started building the bodies for the Cheetahs in the spring of 1939, even Blackpool had to accept that war was inevitable, and that they were likely to have far too many trams and buses. The Corporation managed to postpone delivery of most of their order until 1940, but agreed to take the Cheetahs. All six were licensed at the end of July and some, if not all, went into service in August.

The bus fleet had re-started at No. 1 in 1937, perhaps to avoid overlapping the

tram fleet (only to revert to 200 after the war). So the Cheetahs became Nos. 19 - 24, which was doubly curious since the new saloons, Nos. 13 - 18, didn't arrive until 1940.

On a War Footing

In September 1939, for the second time in 25 years, Blackpool Transport had to switch to a war footing. With the reduction in visitors and the rationing of petrol, the entire fleet of runabouts was withdrawn for the duration - the Lions and Gondolas in 1939 and the new Cheetahs in 1940. However there was other work for some of them.

The Corporation, prompted by the Home Office, had drawn up plans for the defence of Blackpool against German air raids as early as 1935. The task of rescuing victims from bombed buildings was given to the Highways Department, who already had most of the equipment needed, and an adequate supply of manpower accustomed to heavy work. Altogether some 200 men were involved, divided into 18 Rescue Squads, one of which was always standing by at a Rescue Depot. There were two of these, one in the Highways yard at Layton and another in the Cleansing yard on the east side of the railway at Rigby Road.

After the war the Gondolas and Lions were housed on the left-hand tracks of Rigby Road tram depot. These two are 115 and 55, still looking as good as new in September 1949. *(J. Voerman)*

Lions to the Rescue

The nine Lion runabouts (55 - 66, except 58, 59 and 63) which were converted into Rescue buses in December 1939, were kept in the Transport Depot at Rigby Road. If the air-raid siren sounded during the day, Transport Department drivers would immediately take the buses to the two Rescue Depots.

At night the operation was much more difficult. In 1940 there were no two-way radios or mobile telephones, indeed very few telephones at all. Mobilising a force of 200 men from their beds and transporting them to bombed buildings around the town was fraught with problems.

A complex night-time routine was therefore evolved, based on the air-raid siren. In theory this would wake the men, though in exercises some slept through it – or said they had. The men would then go to a variety of rendezvous points round the town.

As soon as the siren sounded, night staff at Rigby Road garage would drive the buses out. The sight and sound of nine streamlined runabouts with twelve-year-old Leyland Lion engines taking off from Rigby Road in convoy must have been like something from the Battle of Britain.

One of the Lions would go directly to each Rescue Depot and the others to the rendezvous points to collect the Rescue Squads. After waiting seven minutes at the pick-up points, the Lions would then race off to the two Depots to receive their instructions, and from there go wherever they were needed.

All this was done only for practice during the Phoney War in early 1940.

Rebuilt Leyland Lion No. 66 in its wartime guise as Rescue vehicle No. 6 in October 1940. The location is thought to be the Rescue Depot in the Highways Yard at Layton.

Ironically the first real use of the Rescue runabouts, on 9 August that year, wasn't an air raid at all, but the collapse of the roof at the new Vickers aircraft factory at Squires Gate, which killed six workmen.

When real air raids on Blackpool started on 2 September 1940, they turned out to be much less devastating than expected. Nevertheless it was decided to convert the three remaining Lions into Rescue vehicles. This wasn't done until the end of October, too late for Blackpool's most serious raid of the war, on 9 September, when a lone German bomber hit North Station,

killing eight people in houses nearby. The single raider wasn't picked up by the warning system, which meant that the much-practised rescue procedure couldn't be invoked. Fortunately the Rescue crew on stand-by at Layton heard the explosions and went directly to the scene.

This turned out to be the runabouts' finest hour, and the only raid which involved real rescue work. Altogether there were 73 alerts in 1940, 58 in 1941 and only four in 1942. In fact, Blackpool's worst incident of the war was another accident, when two RAF planes collided and fell onto Central Station on 27 August 1941, killing eighteen people.

Other towns were less fortunate, and on 14 March 1941 one of the runabouts was despatched to Wallasey to assist in clearing up after a raid on Merseyside. This was an epic journey both for the Lion and for the Rescue squad, on an open bus with no seats and in winter. So it was decided to fit one of the buses (believed to be No. 57) for long-distance working, with shelter and seats for the squad, lockers for blankets, plus a primus stove and kettle for the obligatory pot of tea.

The Lions didn't spend all their time waiting at Rigby Road or racing round the town. On several occasions they appeared in Civil Defence or fund-raising processions along the Promenade, looking quite magnificent in convoy, and no doubt reminding many spectators of happier days.

Buses 60 and 55 (Rescue vehicles 2 and 3) lead another five Leyland Lions along Central Beach during a Civil Defence parade on 26 March 1941.

In December 1939, despite reservations from the Home Office, nine of the Lion runabouts were converted to "Rescue lorries", a simple process of removing the seats, for which Walter Luff charged the Civil Defence Committee a modest 25s. 0d. per bus.

In 1943, the Civil Defence operation was merged with the First Aid Party Service. During the subsequent reorganisation somebody decided that more Rescue buses were needed - even though there hadn't been an air-raid alert since July 1942 - and it seems that Gondolas 114, 115, 116 and 119 were also commandeered. No. 118 had already become a mobile canteen *(page 130)*.

The run-down of the Rescue fleet started in November 1944, when Lions 64 and 66 and the four Gondolas were released. No. 63 followed in December, but the rest of the Lions were kept until the war in Europe ended in May 1945.

However none of the runabouts re-entered service until the following season. Six years of exposure to Rescue crews in hob-nailed boots had no doubt left its mark, and they must have needed a repaint at the very least. Even the 1939 Cheetahs, which were still in virtually mint condition, didn't appear.

Peacetime

When the runabouts at last emerged, during the second week of July 1946, they ran mainly on routes 23 and 24, with occasional trips to Stanley Park. Only the Gondolas and Cheetahs were used. The season ended early, as there were no Illuminations, and by the end of August the buses were back in the depot for the winter. During 1947 the runabouts ran even less than the previous year, but in 1948 they came out at Whit, which was a step in the right direction.

In September 1948, Walter Luff reviewed the state of the bus fleet, and reported that the 24 runabouts were good for at least another five years' service. But it wasn't until the Lights restarted in 1949 that the runabouts really got back into their stride, and again became regular performers on the revived Illuminations Tour.

After the war, the twelve Lions were used only very occasionally at the height of the season. In March 1953, the Transport Committee decided to keep them in case they were needed during the Coronation celebrations in June that year. By July 1953, they were stored, along with the former Gondola, No. 118, in the wartime garage at Bond Street, which functioned as a store for assorted junk or a treasure-house of potential museum pieces, depending on your point of view. Unfortunately the Transport Department's view put the

In 1959 the Transport Department converted double-deckers 26 - 28 to open-top for use on a Circular Tour along the Promenade to Anchorsholme, and back via Stanley Park to South Shore. However because of objections by other operators, the tour never got off the ground, and the open-toppers spent much of their lives on the town routes and the No. 8 service to Stanley Park. This is No. 26 in Church Street during 1960. *(Robert Mack)*

Lions firmly in the first category and they were all sent for scrap in 1954.

The operational runabouts - six Cheetahs and five Gondolas - were stationed in Rigby Road tram depot until 1953, but their glory days were over. The Gondolas ran for the last time in 1955, and were sold for scrap in February 1956, except No. 118, which was by then stored in Marton Depot.

This left only the Cheetahs. Much of their time was spent on the town centre routes and the Illuminations Tour. No. 20 was converted to a one-man vehicle

by moving the entrance to the front, but no more were done, and in 1961 the whole class went for scrap.

After 35 years of Freighters, Guys, Gondolas, Lions and Cheetahs - in peacetime and wartime - it was the end of the runabout bus in Blackpool. Elsewhere the open single-decker managed to survive in a few British resorts, but there hasn't been one in Blackpool since 1961. Which seems a shame for a town which once probably had more of them than anywhere else in the country.

During the Fifties and Sixties, the pre-war Park Circular route made a ghostly reappearance as service 17 for a few days each July when the Royal Lancashire Show was held on the old Stanley Park airport. Buses 291 and 299 are loading at the showground in 1968, the last year the route was operated by Walter Luff's centre-entrance buses. The site is now occupied by Blackpool Zoo. *(Brian Turner)*

Back from the Dead - Gondola Bus 118

Above: Gondola bus 118 was only a few weeks old when it was photographed in the sunshine outside Central Station on 5 August 1935, at the end of another trip on the No. 8 route from Stanley Park. *(Leyland Journal/BCVM)*

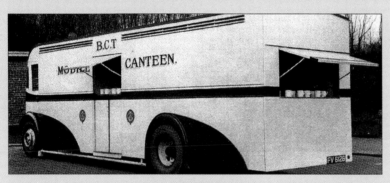

Above: No. 118 after it had been rebuilt by the Transport Department as a mobile canteen early in 1941. *(Passenger Transport Journal)*

Below: Owner Ray Hughes (on the right) with fellow-Gondoliers and the chassis of No. 118, which they are restoring at the St. Helens Transport Museum. *(Brian Turner)*

Between 1935 and 1951, Walter Luff bought a total of 218 streamlined buses for Blackpool. Only one of these distinctive vehicles – the last of all, double-decker No. 300 – has ever been restored to running order, and even that hasn't been seen for many years. However if all goes according to plan, one of Luff's very first streamliners – the magnificent open Gondolas of 1935 – will soon be taking to the road again.

This remarkable story starts in December 1940 when Gondola 118 was officially withdrawn – after running for only five seasons and accumulating an estimated 30,000 miles – to be converted into a mobile canteen, catering for rescue teams working at bomb sites. 118 emerged from Rigby Road for its new rôle in May 1941.

Although the conversion was meant to be reversible, No. 118 was never converted back to an operational bus after the war. But nothing was scrapped in Walter Luff's postwar regime, so 118 hung on, latterly at the back of Marton Depot, even after the rest of the Gondolas went for scrap. 118 survived until May 1961 when it was sold for £26 to a Blackpool man who used it as a café at Waterloo Road car park.

Just what happened next isn't clear, but during the 1980s the remains of 118 were purchased for an abortive attempt at preservation. They finished up at Darwen and there in September 1997 they were about to be sold for scrap.

They were bought by Ray Hughes and his son Robert for £200, as spares for a Lancashire United Transport Lion they were restoring. They had no idea of the significance of what they had bought until the chassis, with a load of body parts, arrived at the St. Helens Transport Museum.

Once the light dawned, and they realised that they now owned the last Blackpool Gondola, the Hughes's quickly reorganised their schedule, and the LUT Lion took a back seat. Examination showed that the Gondola was eminently restorable. The chassis was virtually complete, lacking only a carburettor and starter motor.

The metalwork of the body had largely wasted away, but most of the wooden body frame survived. The major new construction was likely to be the central pagoda. At the time of writing it was estimated that No. 118 would require another two years' work. Few projects promise to add so much to the transport heritage of Britain in general, and Blackpool in particular.

19. Toastracks in Retirement

Above: **TV car 166 near the Tower running back to Rigby Road after a live ABC broadcast of "Holiday Town Parade" on 8 July 1961. 166 is now preserved at the National Tramway Museum.** *(Brian Turner)*

Below: **Toastrack 161 in its wartime guise as a Water Car at Copse Road on 16 April 1947. Soon after this photograph was taken, 161 lost its motors and its fleet livery, and became No. 7 in the works car fleet.** *(National Tramway Museum)*

Chapter Sixteen left the Blackpool toastracks in 1942, at the end of their passenger careers. By then all 24 of the original racks had been broken up, but cars 161 - 166 were too good to scrap, having run less than 50,000 miles each since they were built in 1927. They never ran in service again, but some of them were to lead pretty eventful retirements.

The Water Car, No. 161

The first toastrack to be reincarnated was No. 161, which went into the workshops at Rigby Road in November 1941 to be converted into a Water Tank Car for the Fleetwood section. Most of the seats were removed and two large rectangular tanks mounted on the underframe.

Just why a Water Tank Car was needed wasn't explained. There had never been one before (or since). But it was almost certainly connected with a general instruction issued by the Ministry of War Transport in June 1941 that vehicles should be dispersed overnight to reduce the risk of bomb damage. Blackpool accordingly dispersed buses to Talbot Road bus station and Bond Street, and drew up plans for extending Copse Road Depot at Fleetwood.

Experience of air raids in Britain's cities had shown that some of the worst damage was caused by incendiary bombs, particularly when water mains had been fractured. During 1941 emergency water tanks were built all over Blackpool, and No. 161 must have been part of the arrangements for fire-fighting at Copse Road. In theory, if the overhead wires

were intact, it could have been used on any tram route in Blackpool or Fleetwood where water was needed.

Since two 1,700-gallon tanks of water weighed fifteen tons, compared with three tons for a full load of passengers, No. 161 was given the 70 h.p. motors from toastrack 82, which had been scrapped in September 1941. Perhaps to make 161 rather more useful, a separate order was issued to fit the car with snowploughs. These were presumably the sort of angled boards which the

Blackpool rail-grinders had, rather than the large "V" ploughs fitted onto a pair of Fleetwood Racks each winter.

In May 1944, with the threat of air raids receding, No. 161 was fitted with sprinklers at each end, and thereafter was used for spraying weed-killer along the Tramroad sleeper tracks. However 161 only ran under its own power for another four years before its motors were removed in April 1948. It was said that water leaking from the tanks was damaging the motors. The car was given

Blackpool 166 – Britain's Last Toastrack

There were never many places to ride on a toastrack, but now there is only one – the National Tramway Museum at Crich in Derbyshire.

The museum – with the Corporation's approval – had long since ear-marked one or other of the two TV cars for restoration as a toastrack. So when Blackpool decided that 166 was redundant, museum volunteers quickly stripped the car of its TV accoutrements and what was left – little more than a motorised platform on wheels – arrived at Crich in June 1972.

Restoration

The workshop staff at Crich were pleasantly surprised to receive a tram in such excellent mechanical condition. The toastrack had only run just over 40,000 miles, and apart from some perished cables, its bogies were as good as new. The metal

Top: At the start of its last full season in Blackpool, No. 166 arrives at Bispham tram station on Easter Sunday, 9 April 1939. On the right is the track leading down Red Bank Road to Bispham depot, where several of the toastracks were stored by this time. *(H.B. Priestley, National Tramway Museum)*

Left: Dumped – No. 166 on 21 June 1953, awaiting its rendezvous with the scrapman. All the even-numbered toastracks, 162, 164 and 166 were abandoned on Thornton Gate sidings in 1953. *(R.B. Parr, National Tramway Museum)*

Below: The great survivor – the only tram ever to escape from Thornton Gate. Just eleven weeks after the picture above was taken, No. 166 was back in action, fitted with cameras for its first television broadcast on 10 September 1953. It is seen in Hopton Road, going out on a test run.

tyres had never been turned down and still bore the maker's stamp "1926".

In accordance with their restoration policy, the museum decided to return the car to original 1927 condition with full-width seats. Although 166 had lost many of its seats, it still retained enough cast-iron end-frames to equip the entire tram – 1927 condition only needed half as many frames as 1936 condition, with split seats.

At the time several complete toastrack seats still existed outside the village shop in Weeton, near Blackpool, but the owner refused to part with them. The restorers also tried to obtain some seats from the Llandudno toastracks, which had survived on the Fairbourne Railway in Wales – the seats, not the toastracks – but without success.

Although, as somebody remarked

during the rebuilding, 166's body finished where most tram bodies started, several detailed items still had to be built from scratch, including the wooden parts of the seats and the brass handrails. The destination box and the ornate brackets which supported it were new, as were the blinds, which were based on a genuine example from a toastrack.

Also completely new were the "Circular Tour" destination boards and their supports. On a point of detail, the lettering on the boards should have been red rather than black. This was confirmed quite independently by Bill Latham of the Oxford Hotel *(see page 29)* and Jim Dean, who knew both the Blackpool and Southport toastracks.

The dashes - again new - were painted, lined and numbered to match the bright red 1927 livery which had been revealed by careful rubbing-down of one of the original dashes. Until recently it was assumed that this shade of red had been in use since at least 1911 and that toastracks 69 – 92 had carried it when new.

However when Blackpool works car 754 was being rubbed down at Beamish for restoration as rebuilt Marton Box car 31 in 1988, the red which emerged was a much darker crimson shade than on 166. It seems, therefore, that the brighter red was only adopted in the early Twenties, and that toastracks 69 – 92 originally carried the crimson livery.

Active Retirement

No. 166 entered service at Crich on 18 August 1974, and soon began accumulating between 500 and 700 miles a year, more than it had run altogether during the previous 34 years. In fact 166 was worked nearly as hard at Crich as it had been at Blackpool during the Thirties.

Since arriving at the museum, 166 has had its share of the limelight – certainly more than it ever had during its passenger career at Blackpool. Two years after it was restored, 166 joined the select list of British trams to be driven by royalty, when the Duke of Gloucester visited the museum as patron of the Tramway Museum Society on 9 June 1976.

No. 166 played a central rôle in a more poignant occasion on 9 September 1985, when it bore the coffin of Richard Fairbairn, a lifelong tramway enthusiast who lived at the museum as Security Officer for many years. He had, remarkably, been born at the Worcester horse–tram depot, where his father was manager, in 1895.

When he died, Richard Fairbairn's family found amongst his papers a request that his body "be conveyed by special tramcar over the Society's tramway ... so that I may take final leave of the form of transport with which I have been so closely linked from the moment of my birth."

Above: **H.R.H. the Duke of Gloucester, patron of the Tramway Museum Society, at the controls of 166 on 9 June 1976. Chief Driving Instructor Merlyn Bacon seems confident enough in his royal pupil.** *(David Frodsham)*

Below: **During his visit, the Duke met Richard Fairbairn, the museum's oldest officer, then aged 81. Nine years later No. 166, draped in black and flying a black pennant from its trolley pole, bore Richard Fairbairn's coffin on his last tram ride.** *(David Frodsham)*

No. 165 in Rigby Road Depot, fitted up with television equipment for its historic broadcast on 14 October 1951 - the first transmission from a moving vehicle. *(Dennis Gill)*

the number 7 and painted in the green works-car livery; thereafter it was pulled by the electric locomotive which until 1948 had towed coal wagons from Fleetwood to Thornton Gate sidings.

No. 7 survived until 1957 when it was dumped at Thornton Gate sidings. One of its tanks was removed in May 1959 and fitted onto a four-wheeled truck as a weed-killing trailer, and what remained was eventually towed away to Copse Road for scrap in February 1960.

Cold Storage

Once Marton Depot had been released by the Air Ministry (who had sub-let it to Vickers for aircraft manufacture) in 1945, space was no longer a problem and Walter Luff began to hoard all his redundant trams in Blundell Street and Marton, and his buses at Bond Street, South Shore.

According to Joe Franklin, Luff believed that if the newly-elected Labour Government chose to nationalise public transport, fleet size would be a factor in assessing compensation (or perhaps the status of managers). So the toastracks sat in Blundell Street - still with their wartime headlight masks - alongside rows of dusty Standard cars. In 1949, they were moved to Marton Depot.

The Television Toastrack, No. 165

If 161's function after retirement was unusual, No. 165's was historic. To mark the opening of television broadcasting in the North of England on 12 October 1951, the BBC decided to televise the Illuminations from a tram - the first television programme to be broadcast from a moving vehicle.

The tram chosen for this epic occasion was toastrack 165, still in passenger livery with green V's. 165 had lost its seats as early as 1949, and now they were replaced by an assortment of BBC

paraphernalia, powered by a petrol-engined generator at the rear of the car. In the centre was a "control room", which consisted of a pair of watchmen's huts lashed down to 165's underframe. Just behind the driver was a large platform about four feet high, carrying an extra-sensitive Marconi camera with a single fixed lens - there were no zoom lenses in those days. The BBC's arrangements may have been makeshift, but the Corporation did things in style at the front, with the words "BBC Television" in illuminated letters.

After numerous test runs, the live broadcast took place between South Pier and Bispham on Sunday 14 October. The Transport Department stationed inspectors along the route to keep the path clear for No. 165. The pictures were transmitted from the tram by a

beam aimed manually at the top of Blackpool Tower and from there to the BBC stations at Holme Moss, Sutton Coldfield and Alexandra Palace. Commentary from the tram was relayed by a separate radio link.

Colder Storage

The election of a Conservative government in 1951 removed the threat of nationalisation, and with the imminent arrival of 25 Coronation cars, scrapping of trams recommenced in September 1951.

Only one of the four remaining cars escaped the axe when it fell on the toastracks early in 1953. 163 found a haven at Copse Road, as the basis for a future illuminated car, but 162, 164 and 166 were dumped at Thornton Gate sidings early in 1953 and left there with their trolleys tied down. In December 1954, 162 and 164 were taken back to Rigby Road and scrapped.

The TV Twins, Nos. 165 & 166

The next broadcast of the Lights took place on 10 September 1953. By this time the amount of paraphernalia was so large that a second tram was needed. So toastrack 166 *(page 132)* was rescued from Thornton Gate and adapted as the principal TV car. It kept most of its seats, but had boards mounted over them to carry the cameras - three this time. The producer and commentator sat in an elevated position at the back, looking, as one observer put it, rather like stage-coach guards. Both of them were top BBC men, Barney Colehan and Richard Dimbleby.

165 was relegated to secondary

No. 165, carrying the heavy equipment for the second Illuminations broadcast in September 1953, takes a test run up the Promenade with Norman Wylie at the controls. Coupled behind is toastrack 166, carrying the cameras. *(W.J. Wyse, snr.)*

support vehicle, carrying the heavy gear in two "huts", one for the transmission equipment and the other for a large diesel generator. Both cars still carried green-V livery, but lost their headlights and now had three-line illuminated lettering saying "BBC Television Service" at the outer ends of the set. The two cars ran coupled together, but had their own drivers, each receiving instructions from the producer by headphone. The front car was driven by Norman Wylie of the engineering staff, wearing his customary trilby hat, which offered barely adequate protection on a stormy Blackpool evening.

Whilst the drivers may have been used to braving the elements, the broadcasters and the sound effects microphones suffered from the weather in both 1953 and 1955, so for the 1956 transmission the BBC asked the Transport Department to provide more shelter.

No. 166 was therefore upgraded. The camera position remained in the open air, but the producer and commentator sat in an enclosed cabin at the rear, with curtains and upholstered seats. No. 165 was altered to match, and both cars were repainted cream, losing their V's and their fleet numbers, but keeping the illuminated "BBC Television Service" lettering.

The BBC lost their monopoly in 1955, and ABC Television, the new weekend commercial broadcaster for the north-west, started to use the two TV cars for transmitting variety shows from Blackpool. The illuminated lettering was cunningly modified so that the first "B" could be replaced with an "A" as appropriate. Inevitably in September 1957, both companies wanted the TV cars at the same time, and ABC had to settle for an open Boat instead.

ABC's equipment was more modern than the BBC's, and they didn't always need 165. But the BBC were still using both cars when they televised the Lights for the last time on 2 September 1965.

By then tastes were changing, and the Illuminations broadcast had lost its appeal. The days of the TV toastracks were over, though the Transport Department kept them intact in case the advent of colour television in 1968 revived interest. When the fleet was renumbered in May 1968 to suit the Transport Department's new computer, 165 and 166 became Nos. 16 and 17 in the works car series, but it was obvious that 165 would never be needed again and in July 1968 it was broken up in Blundell Street.

The Blackpool Belle, No. 163

By the late Fifties the only toastrack in anything like original condition was No.

Although it had originally been intended to run the Blackpool Belle regularly on the Promenade Circular, the only time it happened was between 2 and 4 June 1961 when the magazine *Melody Maker* paid £5 an hour for the Belle to run during a jazz festival. *(Brian Turner)*

163 which slumbered, all but forgotten, in Copse Road Depot along with two other relics, Dreadnought 59 and Fleetwood Rack 127. Had 163 stayed there a year longer it might well have been restored with them in 1960.

Instead it was converted into the Blackpool Belle, a new illuminated tram for the 1959 Lights. No. 163 served in that rôle until 1978, by which time it had run just 51,080 miles since it was built – 1,000 miles a year.

Four years later the Belle was bought by the Glenwood trolley museum in Oregon. The car was later transferred to the non-electric Willamette Shore railway where it ran from 1992 to 1994, fitted with a gas engine – shades of the

Lytham gas trams – and a rectifier to provide 550 volts DC.

Extensive alterations were made to enable the Belle to negotiate the line's trestle bridges and tunnels. Most of the top deck was removed, and the roof of each cab was raised six inches, so that the car could be operated by drivers more than six feet tall. Huge 28-inch ship's lights were fixed at each end, as well as a high-density halogen light on the bows.

The Willamette Shore line has since closed and the Blackpool Belle has been retired. It doesn't look a great deal like it used to, which probably doesn't matter too much. But under there somewhere is the world's second surviving toastrack, and it would be a pity to lose it.

The Blackpool Belle in July 1994, somewhat reduced in stature and further dwarfed by the freeway bridges at the northern terminal of the Willamette Shore Line in Oregon. The car behind is San Antonio No. 300. *(PC)*

20. The Blackpool Boat Cars

In much the same way as the original Circular had been transformed by the arrival of the toastracks, so in 1934 the extended Circular Tour was updated by a new fleet of streamlined open single-deckers.

The first new vehicle in Walter Luff's Five Year Plan for the complete transformation of Blackpool's transport system – single-deck "railcoach" No. 200 - arrived from English Electric in June

Above: **A Boat reversing at the Tower in May 1959, with open-top buses 27 and 28 loading for Stanley Park.** *(Robert Mack)*

Opposite: **It wasn't easy to convey the holiday atmosphere in February, but the Fox photographer could have chosen a cheerier location than the corner of Blundell Street and Princess Street. A spare tram crew and some of the staff from the Transport offices, just off picture to the right, are masquerading as passengers on 6 February 1934 for the official portrait of prototype Boat car 225.** *(Fox Photos/HG)*

Below: **H. Viney's Leyland six-tonner towing No. 228, the second Luxury Toastrack of the production batch, along Preston Corporation's Ashton tram route on its way from Strand Road works to Blackpool on 23 July 1934. Vineys had the trailer built specially for delivering centre-entrance cars to Rigby Road.** *(Leyland Journal/BCVM)*

1933, and in August the Corporation ordered 24 more to replace the antiquated Fleetwood Box cars, relics of the original Pilling Tour.

It might have been thought that the Circular Tour and its toastracks would be fairly low on Luff's list of priorities. Perhaps the profitability of the service appealed to his accountant's mind, but one of the first things he did after ordering the railcoaches was to plan replacements for the toastracks.

On 25 September 1933 Luff showed the Transport Committee two large model tramcars - an open-top double-decker to replace the Dreadnoughts and an open single-decker "without the objection of a clinging conductor and steps over the wheels," a modern version of the toastracks. Accompanying the models were quotations from English Electric (who badly needed the business) for two prototype cars, and a production batch of 25 of each type. The Committee were more circumspect and waited to see the prototypes.

The Prototype

The prototype "Luxury Toastrack" duly arrived from Preston during the first week of February 1934. It was based closely on the railcoaches which English Electric had just finished delivering, and took the next number, 225.

According to Corporation records, No. 225 didn't enter service until the start of the summer timetable on Saturday 19 May. This is surprising since a press release on 20 March described 225 as being "ready for the track". The weather at Easter was good enough for the toastracks and Fleetwood Racks to run, and it's hard to believe that 225 didn't make at least a token appearance.

The Production Batch

In March 1934 the Committee approved the production batches of the new cars, but halved the proposed order to eleven toastracks and twelve Dreadnoughts, making 25 cars altogether.

The production toastracks were very similar to No. 225, but had higher sides and a more rounded canopy. The first car, No. 227, arrived at the end of July, taking the next number after the prototype double-decker. The rest followed quickly, to fill the sequence 228 - 237, and the entire class was in service by 12 August. Just before the last car was delivered, the prototype double-decker was renumbered 237, and the final toastrack became No. 226 instead.

The Luxury Toastracks cost £1,573 each, except the first two, 225 and 227, which had second-hand equipment. No. 227 cost £1,375 and 225 probably less (the uncertainty arises because the two prototypes were charged to revenue at £4,170 for the pair).

It wasn't long before the label "Luxury Toastrack" came under scrutiny. The *Evening Gazette* thought that "the new streamlined toastracks are proving especially popular. But can we call them toastracks now? They look too dignified to bear the name of toastrack. Can anybody find a better name? What about Cruisers?" It certainly had more of a ring than the rather prosaic "Boats" which eventually stuck. Ideally they would have been "Gondolas" but the 1925 illuminated car had pre-empted that.

At the end of their first season, one of the Boats returned to English Electric to appear in an exhibition of the company's latest vehicles at Preston works between the 3rd and 8th of December 1934. Other Blackpool exhibits included the last of the open-top double-deckers (No.

Furious - not to say spurious - activity at Marton Depot in May 1939, "painting the familiar open toastracks in readiness for Whitsuntide", according to the original caption on this press photograph. To add human interest the photographer has again conscripted the office staff, here applying an unconvincing paint brush to No. 229. *(Fox Photos)*

The Mystery Tour of 1935

During the summer of 1935 the Boats are believed to have operated briefly on a very unusual tour along the Fleetwood Tramroad. The only authority for the existence of this tour is the late Frank Hirst, who was Rolling Stock Superintendent of the Blackpool Tramways for most of the Walter Luff era, and not a man to imagine such things.

Just how far north this tour went isn't clear, since there were technical and licensing problems running Boats all the way to Fleetwood. However the most interesting part of the route was in Blackpool, where the Boats ran into town along Dickson Road.

Boats on Dickson Road were a great rarity, but the outward route was even rarer. Instead of reversing at Talbot Road terminus, the Boats carried on round the tight right-hand curve onto the Layton route and down Talbot Road into Talbot Square. There they turned right again on the single-track link which brought them onto the northbound Promenade track. Then they were back on familiar ground.

This Circular route was not apparently successful – hardly surprising since it's difficult to see what the attraction was to anybody but a tram enthusiast. It probably only ran for a few weeks, and the only other evidence that it ever existed is a photograph showing (just) a Boat going south on

Boats never normally operated along Dickson Road to North Station. This photograph of No. 229 was taken during an enthusiasts' tour on 13 June 1954. The Mystery Tour of 1935 – if it ever existed – would have continued past the camera and turned right down Talbot Road. Five days after this photograph was taken, Walter Luff retired, and his successor Joe Franklin took an instant dislike to Luff's flamboyant livery - and to his centre-entrance buses. *(Robert Mack)*

Dickson Road, which is believed to have been taken in July 1935.

Frank Hirst recalled that the Boats had problems negotiating the sharp right-hand turn into Talbot Road, where they overhung the track, and this was one reason for the Tour finishing. This route through the town centre had been operated once before, when the track in Dickson Road was being relaid in the winter of 1922/23. For several

months Fleetwood cars ran into town along Dickson Road and out via the Promenade. The Fleetwood trams didn't have the same overhang as the Boats, which may have made a difference.

All this is still supposition, of course, but the odd mystery now and then does add a touch of spice. And some evidence may yet turn up to make the Mystery Tour a mystery no longer.

This may be the mystery tour which Frank Hirst recalled – not double-decker No. 242 at the Gynn, but the Boat car heading up Dickson Road. The date is probably July 1935.

It's 5.50 p.m. on 23 July 1961, and Boat 228 arrives back at Marton Depot. A railcoach bound for Talbot Square has been waiting while 228 crossed onto the southbound track, ready to reverse again into the right-hand side of the shed. Not a great deal had changed in the fifty years since the photograph on page 21 was taken. *(Brian Turner)*

249), the first of the new enclosed double-deckers (eventually to be No. 258) and an unidentified railcoach. The four Blackpool cars apparently stayed at Preston until April 1935.

In Service

The new Boats soon settled down to accumulate around 7,000 miles a year. They were heavily used during the Illuminations, when their trolley towers carried translucent designs with a wind-driven mechanism inside providing a change of colour.

Like the toastracks, the Boats could run on any route, though there's no record of them (or any other streamlined car) running on the Layton or Central Drive routes which closed in October 1936.

It seems that No. 225 was the first to venture to Fleetwood, but not until 3 August 1937. Running on the Tramroad required a special tyre profile - which 228 was given in July 1938, 226 in September 1939, 233 in August 1941 and 227 at some unknown date - and each car had to be licensed by Fleetwood Council.

As late as 1947 only five Boats (225 - 228 and 233) had Fleetwood licences, but rules were made to be broken, and on 6 August 1947, car 234 was caught red-handed in a spot-check at Fleetwood. By 1949 all the Boats had Fleetwood licences, though it was still unusual to see one there. In fact the Boats had become much less visible all

round since the Circular Tour finished in 1940. Their annual mileage fell drastically, from 7,000 before the war to around 2,000.

New Livery

It wasn't until the Circular Tour was resurrected in 1957 that the Boats returned to the limelight. They took this revived activity in their stride, but their drivers didn't. The old school of weather-beaten tram drivers - accustomed to battling through the winter with no more protection than cap, greatcoat, gauntlets and occasionally goggles - had disappeared. Tram drivers of the Fifties were much less happy to have the wind in their face, even in summer. In June 1958, No. 227 appeared with experimental perspex windscreens, and the rest of the Boats followed suit during the next winter.

The windscreens didn't do much for the pleasing lines of the Boats, but the next change did even less. The new manager, Joe Franklin, had developed a deep resentment of the legacy he had inherited from Luff - particularly 25 recently-delivered Coronation cars and 100 centre-entrance double-deck buses.

This grievance manifested itself in a strong dislike of the sweeps and flares with which Luff had made the Blackpool livery so distinctive, albeit a trifle dated. Franklin called them "moustaches" and got rid of them as quickly as he could, starting in October 1954.

It was fitting that the Boats, which

had been the first trams to wear the green-V livery, were eventually the last. Because of their sheltered life-style, the Boats' paintwork lasted longer than average, and they all retained the V until November 1959 when No. 236 was painted all cream. It was not an improvement. The "bow wave" at the front had been an integral part of the design, and without it No. 236 looked graceless and clumsy. Over the next two years, the rest of the moustaches disappeared. No. 230 was the last to be repainted, in the spring of 1962.

The repainting programme was to have sinister implications for the Boats. The cars painted in 1959 (236) and 1961/62 (226, 227, 228, 230 and 235) were given bogie overhauls for the first time, having accumulated about 80,000 miles since new.

For some reason the Boats repainted during 1960 (225, 229, 231, 232, 233 and 234) weren't overhauled. 233 didn't need it, having inherited overhauled bogies from a railcoach in 1945, and 225 later received similar treatment in 1964. No-one realised at the time, but this was to determine the fate of the other four 1960 repaints.

Wanderings

The announcement in 1960 that the street tramways were to close meant that the Boats would have to leave their traditional home at Marton Depot. In 1961 some were moved to Rigby Road (the actual cars varied from time to time), and after Marton closed in 1963, all twelve were stored in the re-opened shed at Blundell Street.

Then nine of them moved again, this time to completely new territory at Bispham Depot, the old headquarters of the Fleetwood Tramroad. They ran from there in 1963, most of them with normal fixed-head trolleys in place of the swivel heads they had needed for the curvaceous Marton route. The remaining three cars (228, 230 and 236) ran from Blundell Street, still with swivel heads.

The cars at Bispham stayed there after the depot closed as a running shed in October 1963, and ran occasionally from Bispham during 1964 - an intriguing throw-back to the Thirties when toastracks had been stored at Bispham and brought out only on the busiest days.

The closing of the subsidiary depots and reorganisation of Rigby Road (with all the attendant scrapping and shuffling of trams) continued into 1965, so the Boats still weren't secure. That summer, eight of the Boats ran from Blundell Street Depot, leaving the four cars which hadn't been overhauled (229, 231, 232 and 234) unused at Bispham. However when Bispham Depot was cleared in October 1965, all four were moved down to Blundell Street and the entire class stored on tracks 1 and 2.

Withdrawals

It looked as if the Boats' wanderings were over, and that they were safely under one roof again, but it wasn't so. The four stragglers from Bispham never ran again. Early in 1968, with space at a premium, it was decided to take them to Thornton Gate sidings and burn them, but in the end they were broken up in Blundell Street between April and August

234 meets its end inside Blundell Street depot in April 1968. Behind 234 is television toastrack 165, which suffered the same fate four months later. 166 at the back of the line managed to escape - the second time Britain's last toastrack had cheated the scrapman. *(Brian Turner)*

1968. Many of the salvaged fittings, like the handles on the driver's doors (rarely used on the Boats), were as good as new.

As if to obliterate the identity of the four lost Boats, the tram fleet was renumbered in May 1968. The eight remaining Boats became 600 to 607, appropriately the lowest numbers in the fleet for the oldest trams.

Emigration

In 1971, No. 601 (ex-226) began to steal the limelight. In February it was fitted with a pantograph borrowed from ex-Sunderland car 100 at Crich - the first pantograph used at Blackpool since 1933. It's not known how far the car ran with

the pantograph, if at all. It certainly didn't run in service; in fact it made its last passenger trip during the first week of August 1970.

In August 1971, 601 sailed from Liverpool through the Panama Canal to San Francisco, where it was due to operate on the Market Street tramway as part of British Week in October. Unfortunately because of a dock strike, 601 was diverted to the Rio Vista trolley museum.

Next to cross the Atlantic, in February 1976, was No. 603, which was "hired" for a silver dollar to the Philadelphia tramways for the American Bicentennial celebrations. 603 lost its trolley tower, but gained folding steps and a trolley retriever, and ran in Philadelphia carrying a special white and orange livery from 6 August 1976.

After running in Philadelphia again in 1977, No. 603 surprisingly returned to Blackpool in July 1978. Nobody seemed to know what to do with it, as Philadelphia had altered the bogies by six inches to the Pennsylvania gauge of 5 ft. 2½ ins., but hadn't changed them back.

Then, just as surprisingly as 603 had returned, in February 1985 it set off back across the Atlantic again, this time to the West Coast. It was bought by the San Francisco Municipal Railway to replace No. 226, which they had borrowed from Rio Vista and operated on the Market Street tramway between 1983 and 1985 as part of a Vintage Trolley Festival whilst the city's cable tramways were being rebuilt. The festival was so popular that it became an annual event, and eventually the line along Market Street

603 enjoys the sunshine during a rare winter outing at the Chestnut Hill terminus in Philadelphia during the 1976 Bicentennial celebrations. Alongside is Toronto car 2242. *(R.E. Jackson)*

Slow Boat to California

Top: Boat 226, renumbered 601 in May 1968, was the first of its class to be preserved. It last ran in Blackpool in August 1970. Here it is making a rare journey on the declining Promenade Circular on 11 July 1969. *(Stephen Holt)*

Centre: On 19 August 1971, 601 left Blackpool via the Panama Canal for San Francisco, where it was due to operate during British Week. Unfortunately a dock strike prevented it being unloaded, and 601 was diverted to the trolley museum at Rio Vista, in the California desert 50 miles north-east of San Francisco. It was 1983 before 601, now 226 again, reached San Francisco for the Trolley Festival which ran whilst the cable car system was being rebuilt. This is Market Street on 24 June 1983. The wires are too low for the Boat's normal trolley tower. *(Bill Owyang, San Francisco Public Utilities Division)*

Below: The San Francisco Municipal Railway later bought Boat car 603 (228) from Blackpool, and returned 226 to Rio Vista. It runs there on a fragment of the great Sacramento Northern, America's longest electric interurban line, which once ran for 200 miles northwards from San Francisco. Here 226 basks in the California sunshine on 10 September 1995, whilst a classic wooden interurban car, Petaluma & Santa Rosa No. 63, loads for another run down the main line. *(Brian Turner)*

was transformed into an all-day, all-year tramway service operated by historic cars.

Nadir of the Boats

With the departure of 601 and 603, the original twelve Boats were now reduced to six. The survivors still saw very little use, averaging only around 500 miles a year between 1975 and 1980.

In August 1983 the Boats reached rock bottom. Because of a shortage of trolley poles, 600, 604, 606 and 607 were cannibalised to keep the rest of the fleet running, and didn't - couldn't - operate again for two years. 602 was similarly emasculated early in 1984, leaving 605 as the solitary Boat running that summer.

The trolleys were restored for the Tramway Centenary in 1985, but only four of the six survivors reappeared, the other two Boats being temporarily swapped for cars from museum operators. 607, along with Balloon 710, was loaned to the National Tramway Museum in exchange for Standard car 40 and Pantograph 167. During the summer, No. 607 ran 1,056 miles at Crich - twice its usual mileage in Blackpool - but returned to Blackpool in December and was back on the Promenade in 1986.

No. 600, the prototype Boat, was sent to the Heaton Park museum tramway in exchange for Manchester 765. Its trolley tower had to be removed so that it could fit into the restricted depot at Heaton Park. When 765 was sent back, 600 didn't return to Blackpool, and wasn't to see the Tower again for another thirteen years.

Revival

With only one car running in 1984 and four in 1985, the Boats were beginning to look like an endangered species, particularly when they ran their last recorded Promenade Circulars in June 1986.

But gradually the picture changed. The revival started with the Glasgow Garden Festival in 1988. Transport within the Festival site was provided by a specially-built tramway operated by preserved cars, plus Boat No. 606, painted in a blue and yellow advertising livery. Intriguingly there was just a hint of a moustache about 606, with the mouldings for the old bow-wave picked out in white. 606 was back in Blackpool for the 1989 season, still in advertising livery, but the advertisements were overpainted blue in July and later replaced with slogans for the Fylde Coast Rover ticket.

Turning out 606 in blue and yellow seems to have inspired the Paint Shop,

Boat car 607 spent the summer of 1985 at the National Tramway Museum, along with Balloon 710, in exchange for cars from Crich which were featuring in the Blackpool Centenary celebrations. Behind 607 on 18 May is steam tram engine "John Bull", which paid a fleeting visit to Blackpool, operating on the Promenade only for the day of the centenary itself - 29 September 1985. *(David Frodsham)*

and during the winter of 1989/90, they set about the remaining Boats with a vengeance. It was not before time, as most hadn't been painted since the early Seventies.

First to appear at the beginning of December 1989 was 602, wearing the rather funereal black and yellow livery of Blackpool Transport's minibus fleet. The most notable feature of the repaint was the restoration of the full "bow wave" in black against the yellow. Moustaches were back.

602 was striking enough, but No. 604 looked simply magnificent when it emerged from the Paint Shop two weeks later in Blackpool's traditional red and white livery, as applied to the fleet of ex-London Routemaster buses.

The third repaint was in some ways the best of all. No. 605, out of action since May 1987, was put in good order with financial support from the Fylde Tramway Society, and appeared at the end of April 1990 in its original 1934 green-V livery.

Modifications

These splendid new liveries weren't the only changes to the Boats. The perspex windscreens fitted in 1959 had become badly scratched and drivers complained of poor visibility when the Boats ran at night. In October 1989 the old screens were removed, and those Boats which operated during the rest of the 1989 Illuminations ran without windscreens.

A new and more substantial type of

Just the outline of a moustache on Boat 606 inside the tram depot at the 1988 Glasgow Garden Festival. *(Brian Turner)*

screen was developed, using car 605, which had been out of service since May 1987, as a test-bed. The new design used flat safety glass, but otherwise was pleasantly rounded and suited the Boat profile surprisingly well. Screens were fitted to the rest of the class during the winter of 1989/90.

During the Boat resurgence, No. 607 was still running in its plain cream Sixties livery, like some ghostly reminder of that dismal period. It was 1996 before 607 too received a repaint with moustaches, this time promoting Travelcards in a green and yellow livery - not the most appealing combination, but representing Blackpool Transport's two liveries. Even after its repaint, and more than ten years since it ran at Crich, 607 still carried a notice warning drivers not to use the trolley reverser at Town End terminus.

In terms of mileage the Boats in the Nineties averaged about 1,200 miles a year, with a peak of over 2,000 in the glorious summer of 1995. To set this in context, the double-deck cars and railcoaches ran about 12,500 miles a year and the Centenary cars (641 – 648) over 30,000.

600 Returns

The Boats' rehabilitation was completed in April 1998, when No. 600, returning belatedly from Heaton Park, was superbly restored to 1934 livery, and fitted with the new style of windscreen. It hadn't run in Blackpool for 16 years.

The renascent 225 rather outshone the Boats which had been re-liveried in

No. 600 ran at Manchester's attractive Heaton Park museum tramway from 1985 to 1998. On 11 May 1986, the Boat's driver collects the single-line staff from Fleetwood Box car 40, with the tram depot in the background. These tracks were once part of the Manchester Corporation Tramways. *(Brian Turner)*

1989, and during the winter of 1998/99 three of them returned to the Paint Shop for another "make-over". First to emerge was No. 606 carrying the blue and yellow livery of the associated Seagull Coaches fleet, followed by 605 in a reversed version of the green-V livery and 602, again in black and yellow.

On 28 June 1998, during the celebrations for the Fleetwood Tramroad

Centenary, No. 600 was one of a handful of trams (607 was another) which ran a special service along Princess Street and Blundell Street. It was uncanny to watch 600, full of passengers, rounding the corner into Blundell Street just as it had done sixty-four years earlier for photographs which appeared in newspapers all over Britain.

If Only ...

It's still hard to think of the Boats as veterans. The design is as timeless and attractive as ever, particularly with the bow waves restored. If only they could take us round the Circular Tour again - the real one, that is.

But that's only one of a dozen "if onlys". If only we could ride through Bodafon Fields on a Llandudno toastrack. If only we could ride to the Giant's Causeway or across the Isle of Bute "to the sands of Ettrick Bay". Perhaps climb to Race Hill on top of a Brighton Tourist Car with the Special Conductor "doing his best to interest and amuse us". Down the 1-in-10 to Scarborough's Aquarium, or through the manicured shrubberies of Southend's suburban Boulevards.

Really, though, we should be thankful for how much has survived. Thankful that we can still travel along Blackpool Promenade on an open tram; still follow the course of the Pilling Tour to Fleetwood; still ride on a Blackpool toastrack. Thankful, in short, that we can still recapture something from the golden age of Seaside Pleasure Riding by Tram.

Not a bad way to go home from school. Red and white Boat car 604 passes Rossall Beach on 7 July 1998 whilst working the afternoon school run from Ash Street, Fleetwood - an unusual duty for a Boat. It is perhaps fitting that the final picture in this book should show a car from Blackpool's Circular Tour running on the only section of the Fleetwood Tramroad which still looks much as it did in the heyday of the Pilling Tour nearly a hundred years before. *(Brian Turner)*

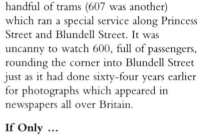